Developing an Ionic Edge

HTML5 Cross Platform Hybrid Apps

Here are the true identities of the Hybrid Collective:
Robin van Baalen, Alan Levicki, Keith D. Moore, Diego Netto, Anton Shevchenko

Developing an Ionic Edge

ISBN 9781939902160

Published by: Bleeding Edge Press, Santa Rosa, CA 95404

Title: Developing an Ionic Edge

Authors: Robin van Baalen, Alan Levicki, Keith D. Moore, Diego Netto, Anton Shevchenko

Editor: Troy Mott

Copy Editor: Christina Rudloff

Typesetter: Bob Herbstman

Cover Designer: Martin Murtonen

Website: bleedingedgepress.com

Table of Contents

Preface

With a powerful framework built on AngularJS at its core, Ionic helps developers build rich, robust hybrid mobile applications. With an emphasis on native performance, Ionic plays nice with Apache Cordova to build native-like hybrid mobile applications for both Android and iOS platforms. It even provides its own wrapping command-line interface (CLI) in order to build, test, and deploy Cordova-based mobile applications.

With tons of popular mobile components, typography, and a gorgeous and extendable base theme, Ionic has been designed to work and display beautifully and *consistently* on all current mobile devices.

The first alpha release of Ionic was made public in late 2013. While this first release was mainly focused on iOS support, the creators made it very clear from the beginning that they wanted the same performance and behavior on both iOS and Android. After many beta releases and breaking changes, Ionic has released v1.0 RC, which covers both iOS and Android, and we have used it for this book and to create our sample Trendicity application.

Why use Ionic?

Have you ever found yourself building a mobile application, but essentially duct taping together common components such as a side menu, modals, tabs, and buttons? Or perhaps you have used a mobile-first framework like Twitter Bootstrap that just doesn't cover enough of what you need? Or perhaps you've already built a great mobile application in your desktop browser, only to find yourself stuck with a slow performing application that relies on many DOM manipulations on your devices?

If you answered yes to any of the above questions, you know why you should use Ionic. At its core, with the powerful AngularJS framework and a focus on native performance, Ionic is your first go-to library when developing a cross platform mobile application. Many issues like scrolling behavior, long list performance, and tap detection are already taken care of, allowing you to focus on developing your application without the headache of cross platform compatiblity issues.

What should readers know prior to reading this book?

Before reading this book, you should have at least a basic knowledge of web (application) development in general, including HTML, CSS, and JavaScript. For a better understanding of our example code and Ionic's features, it is required that the reader has a solid understanding of JavaScript in general and basic knowledge of common AngularJS specific terms.

You won't find a comprehensive reference to AngularJS-specific features or design patterns in this book.

Source code/sample app

For this book, we, the authors, have developed a demo application for you to play around with and as a reference to the mentioned techniques and features of Ionic.

The application is open source and available for free to anyone. Just head over to **https://github.com/trendicity/trendicity** and get your hands dirty with the source code, or directly clone the repository with git:

```
git clone https://github.com/trendicity/trendicity.git
```

What will this book teach you?

In this book, we take you through the process of starting, developing and customizing a mobile application built with the Ionic framework and AngularJS. We start with covering some essential productivity tools such as the Ionic CLI. From there we dive into the development of Trendicity, the mobile application we developed to demonstrate as much of Ionic's features as possible.

Development environment, tooling, and workflow

It's important to first get you started with the required and recommended tools and workflow for this and any future Ionic projects. The most important prerequisites such as installing Node.js, Git, and Ionic CLI are covered. Some generic uses of the Ionic CLI are detailed, and we start off by setting up our demo application project, Trendicity, using front end power tools like Gulp and Bower.

Trendicity

We'll start off by lining out the actual Trendicity demo application. All views will be covered, and some core Ionic UI elements are mixed together to create a basic setup. From handling sidemenu madness to integrating a tab view inside of a nested view, this chapter has got you covered. In Trendicity, a user will be able to set up some favorite locations, check nearby Instagram posts on a map, or open up the previously defined favorites to check out Instagram posts in that area.

Setting up the application routes and implementing the side menu

After we have outlined the big picture of Trendicity, we dive straight in and start working with some of the most commonly used Ionic directives. We discuss the side menu related directives, how to use them, and what they can do for your application. An honorable mention goes out to the `menu-close` directive, which allows you to easily toggle the sidemenu upon navigation. After discussing the side menu directives in detail, we continue on to lay out the application's routing using Angular UI's Router component. This is one of the few external components Ionic Framework depends upon. In the end we take a short peek at what the future of application routing in AngularJS will bring us.

Storing favorite locations in Trendicity

What is a location-based application without favorite locations to store? Next in the book, we discuss how you can use the browser's local storage to store collections of data to allow users to save their favorite locations. Using Ionic's modal service, the user will be able to fill out an address as a favorite location, which will be saved as a favorite location. Behind the scenes, the tailor-made `GeolocationService` are setup to convert that address to a geolocation object using the Google Maps API.

Integrating a map view with Ionic

Integrating a map view in your project in general is by now a pretty straight forward task for most developers. There are many libraries out there that specialize in integrating maps into a project. But doing so within an Ionic project needs a little extra attention due to Ionic's home-made tap/click handling. Of course the team behind Ionic has you covered, and that's how we are able to integrate the open source `angular-google-maps` library into the project.

Authentication

Once we have most features in place, it is time to think about some security in our application. Most of the Trendicity application is freely usable without an account, but once a user starts interacting more with Instagram, it is time for some solid authentication. That's where incorporating the `angular-http-auth` library comes in. We explain how we secured Trendicity with HTTP interceptors and OAuth authentication using the `angular-http-auth` library.

Designing the application

Working with a framework such as Ionic is great. It is a way for you as a developer to create fast prototypes and proof of concept mobile applications, which are based upon a robust framework that allows you to easily edit its look and feel. Customization can be accomplished by using Sass, a powerful CSS extension language that adds some nice extra features to CSS, which we cover in this section of the book.

Creating an Instagram service

Most compelling mobile web applications integrate with some type of backend service. Trendicity integrates with Instagram through the Instagram API. In this chapter, we'll cover everything you need to know to get started with it. This includes everything from OAuth authentication, to installing required Cordova plugins, and building the views with Ionic to display the received data. Every aspect of the Model-View-Controller pattern is covered in this chapter.

What's next?

In the end we look into the future of hybrid application development, AngularJS, and Ionic. Drifty has some exciting new features and products for Ionic on its roadmap, which we will discuss in this chapter. Their Ionic Creator product, and Ionic as a platform, promise to be of great value when developing applications based in Ionic.

The writing process

This book was written by five developers as a book sprint over the course of roughly four months. Especially with a topic like Ionic, which has been subject to constant change over its first year of development, this process has helped to keep the book's content accurate and up-to-date. Conventional books often lag behind the coverage of cutting edge trends and technology due to longer writing and production timelines.

Authors

Anton Shevchenko is a Web Developer at OSEDEA, building scalable enterprise web applications and mobile solutions for businesses. Currently studying Honours Computer Science at the University of Waterloo, Anton enjoys writing code, contributing to the open source community, biking, and watching Apple presentations, preferably all at the same time.

Robin van Baalen is a Dutch software developer with a passion for micro teams having macro ambitions. Working at Neverwoods in Curaçao, Robin works on AngularJS-based web applications with PHP backends and hybrid mobile applications for clients varying from local insurance companies to international banks. To combine his affection for web technologies with the island life, he can be found kitesurfing in the St. Jorisbay when *AFK* (away from the keyboard) on a windy day. You can send him a tweet @biinjo or 'read his mind' at **http://forwebonly.com**.

Keith D. Moore is an independent, full-stack mobile and web application developer/architect. Keith has experience working with a variety of languages and technologies in several industries and domains. He is passionate about solving problems for his clients (at **http://kdmooreconsulting.com**) using the latest and greatest technologies. While not solving all the world's problems, Keith enjoys spending time with his wife, Tracey, his son, Kolton, and his daughter, Ashlyn.

As a software consultant and open source evangelist, **Diego Netto** wears the many hats of a full stack engineer and entrepreneur. Founder of **http://vqtek.com**, a software development agency operating out of Los Angeles and Dallas, Diego helps both startups and Fortune 500 companies leverage the power of open source technologies to deliver intuitive and disruptive products. In his spare time, Diego enjoys participating in various watersports and helps run a boat chartering company.

Alan Levicki is a technical lead and architect that has worked for major motion picture studios and led teams of engineers to build engaging experiences. He is passionate about technology, beer, and bourbon. He is currently located in Austin, TX and can be found on Twitter **@alevicki**.

Acknowledgments

Anton would like to thank Martin Coulombe for introducing him to Ionic. He is also thankful for his family's support throughout the years.

Robin wants to thank his uncle René van Zon for introducing him to web development at the age of 8, and his friend and mentor Felix Langfeldt who always keeps pushing him towards the cutting edge of web technology.

Keith would like to thank his parents for sending him to college to pursue his passion for developing software. He would also like to thank his wife and kids for their support while writing this book.

We would also like to the thank the following technical reviewers for their early feedback and careful critiques: Wesley Cho, Christopher Cook, Andre Dublin, Damian Garzon, Dominik Schreiber, Jamie Sutherland, Jacek Tomaszewski, and Michael Ebo Turkson.

Introduction 1

The mobile application industry is flourishing in the 21st century. Hardware is getting better, and software capabilities have increased exponentially on the small devices we carry around with us every day. The demand for mobile applications has never been higher, and developers are struggling to create enticing experiences on all major platforms to reach the broadest market of people.

The most prevalent approach towards tackling this coveted task is to build native applications. This method requires a deep understanding of various computer languages, most notably Objective-C and Swift for iOS, as well as Java for Android development. Moreover, developers need to be comfortable with using various frameworks and platform-specific SDKs to generate their applications. Needless to say, this strategy comes with challenges and can become very costly when trying to target multiple devices at once.

Hybrid development, on the other hand, is a cost-effective approach for building multi-platform applications. In essence, hybrid applications are mobile-friendly web applications wrapped in a native container application. This structure allows you to develop using HTML5, CSS3, and JavaScript, without having to interact with native platform-specific code. Many developers have been taking advantage of this new approach in order to cope with the growing demand of mobile applications built to run on multiple platforms. Since the advent of the smartphone, numerous frameworks have been created with the sole purpose of facilitating the development of this new type of application. Sencha Touch, Kendo UI, and jQuery mobile are just some of the growing number of mobile-friendly frameworks. There are also frameworks for manipulating the DOM, namely Facebook's React library and Google's AngularJS. In addition, Bootstrap, Foundation, and Topcoat serve to help you with designing your hybrid applications.

In this vast sea of frameworks, it becomes hard to choose the best combination for developing your applications. Most of these frameworks are not well optimized for the hardware limitations of mobile devices and can cause compatability issues when used alongside each other. This is where Ionic comes in.

Ionic

Drifty, the company behind Ionic, is a team of talented developers and designers. The company has created successful projects in the past such as Jetstrap, an interface builder for Bootstrap, and Codiqa, an online drag-and-drop tool for building hybrid applications and mobile websites. Drifty's current mission is to significantly change the future of mobile software development, specifically by improving hybrid mobile application development through Ionic's product offerings.

Ionic combines the strength of Apache's Cordova platform, AngularJS, and Angular UI Router, with its own developed application structure, components, and style sheets. In essence, Ionic takes care of integrating the best mobile frameworks, letting you focus on developing your application's functionality and design without complication.

Built on top of Cordova, Ionic opens up access to scores of Cordova plugins, which act as handlers for various native functionality such as accessing the device's camera, photos, and geolocation, just to name a few. Moreover, the platform lets you create push notifications, and capture device motion/orientation, essentially blurring the lines between native and hybrid application functionality.

What's more, Ionic's decision to integrate AngularJS gives you access to the plethora of functionality attributed to the latter framework. It is a great structural decision, as it compels you to organize code into controllers, services, and directives. Finally, having AngularJS allows you to choose from countless modules created by the open source community, allowing you to extend the core Ionic functionality. For instance, for our Trendicity application we integrated the popular `angular-local-storage` module to store favorite Instagram posts on mobile devices.

Furthermore, Ionic has been greatly focused on the open source community. Not only is the framework itself open source, but the team behind it also created detailed documentation as well as hosted a collection of helpful code samples on CodePen. A public forum serves as a great resource pool to communicate with other developers of the community and allows for interaction with the Ionic team directly.

In the following chapters, we will be stepping through the creation process of our Trendicity application built using Ionic. In addition, we will dive into the range of development possibilities that Ionic allows for when building hybrid mobile applications.

Development environment, tooling, and workflow 2

In this chapter, we cover everything you need in order to get up and running with an Ionic project. You'll install the basic building blocks for an Ionic project, learn how to use the Ionic command line tools to help you initialize a project, learn to add different platforms and plugins, and discover how to test things locally in a browser, on an emulator, and on a real device.

Installing prerequisites: Node.js and Git

Ionic uses the powerful module repository that Node.js offers. Node.js is a JavaScript-based platform that makes building web applications easy. Ionic takes advantage of the nearly ubiquitous nature of Node.js and Node Package Manager (NPM) to ease installation and development.

Installing Node.js

Node.js can be installed by downloading the installer for Windows or OS X located here **nodejs.org/download/**. Node.js can also be installed on OS X via Homebrew. If you are unfamiliar with Homebrew, then you should use the Nodejs.org download link above. Otherwise, you can execute the command:

```
$ brew install node
```

Once installed, you can verify your installation by opening a command prompt and typing:

```
$ node
```

It will bring up a console prompt. This is similar to the JavaScript console located in the browser. You can write valid JavaScript into this console. Try writing:

```
> console.log('Hello World');
```

You should see the output:

```
> console.log('Hello World');
Hello World
undefined
```

To exit the Node.js console press CTRL+C twice.

Installing Git

What NPM is for Node.js dependencies, Bower is for browser dependencies. Because Ionic is an HTML5-based suite of tools and services for mobile hybrid application development, Bower simplifies the process of installing and managing dependencies. Some Bower modules require Git, so you must install Git before you get started.

An installer for Git can be downloaded for all platforms here: **git-scm.com/downloads**.

Once you have installed Git, open a terminal and type:

```
$ git version
```

You should see output similar to the following:

```
git version 1.9.3 (Apple Git-50)
```

Installing Ionic

Now that you have installed Node.js and Git, installing Ionic is a breeze. Open up a terminal and type:

```
$ npm install -g cordova ionic
```

This line is telling NPM to install the `cordova` and `ionic` packages, and any modules they depend upon. The `-g` option means that NPM should install them globally, so that they are available to all projects.

Once NPM is done, it will output a summary of what was installed. You will verify the installation below.

Cordova

It is worth taking some time to explain what Cordova is, since it is a large part of what powers Ionic.

Cordova is a community-driven open source project that bridges the gap between HTML and native phone capabilitiies. This allows developers to build HTML-based applications that can take full advantage of a phone's native functionality like the camera, geolocation, and device orientation. In addition, Cordova attempts to make the interface consistent across different types of devices so that your HTML-based application does not need to know if you are on an iPhone, or an Android device.

You can learn more about Cordova here: **cordova.apache.org/**.

Ionic Command Line Interface (CLI)

In order to make your life easier, Ionic comes with a command line interface that allows you to:

- Start a new project
- Add platforms
- Add plugins
- Build and emulate your project
- Run your project on a real device
- Generate icons and splash page

Starting a new project

Let's create a new project. Open a terminal to a location that you would like to keep your code for this book. Note that the following command will create the application in the directory that you specify.

```
$ ionic start trendicity tabs
```

The `ionic start` command supports specifying a template to use to build the initial structure of your Ionic application. In the previous example, you specified the `tabs` template. Out of the box, Ionic supports blank (the default if none is specified), tabs, and sidemenu. In addition, you can specify a CodePen URL if you want to provide a custom template.

Once Ionic is done setting up your project, you should see the following:

```
Your Ionic project is ready to go!
```

You'll then see some quick tips. It is worth noting that at any time, you can type:

```
$ ionic --help
```

This will show you a list of commands that the Ionic CLI supports.

Take a look at what the command has created for you.

```
$ cd trendicity
$ ls -F
bower.json    gulpfile.js    ionic.project    plugins/
www/
config.xml    hooks/         package.json     scss/
```

- bower.json: Manages your Bower dependencies
- gulpfile.js: Gulp is a build tool. More information about it can be found here **gulpjs.com/**. This file manages the build flow.
- ionic.project: Ionic project configuration
- plugins/: Directory where Ionic installs plugins. You will learn more about these plugins later.
- www/: Your application code
- config.xml: Configuration file for Cordova
- hooks/: Hooks for Cordova
- package.json: Manages your Node.js dependencies
- scss/: SASS files

At this point, let's focus on the `www` directory.

```
$ cd www
$ ls -F
css/        img/        index.html    js/        lib/
templates/
```

css/: Your application's CSS files img/: Any images your application requires index.html: The entry point for your application js/: Your Java-

Script code lib/: Third-party libraries and the Ionic library templates/: HTML templates for sections of your application

Inside of the **js** directory you will find three files: app.js, controllers.js, and services.js.

app.js: Entry point for your application, it contains the routing information. controllers.js: All of the controllers for the example application services.js: Reusable services for the application.

It is worth noting that this is a simplified project structure, and as your application grows, you may need to evolve past it.

Developing in the browser

Initially, it will be much faster for you to test your application in a browser instead of through emulation or on a device. This is possible because Ionic is an HTML5-based platform, meaning it works just fine in a browser. In addition, Ionic has built-in capabilities to make this as simple as possible. Type the following into your terminal from the base directory of your project:

```
$ ionic serve
```

This will open a browser window and serve your Ionic application. Congratulations, you're now up and running!

Note that if a browser window did not open automatically, Ionic informs you of the URL that you need to open in order to view your application. Look for the output in the terminal for:

```
Running dev server: http://localhost:8100
```

You can then open a browser to the URL specified above, to view your application.

This command will monitor the files in your project so that when you change them the view will be refreshed automatically. You can see this by modifying one of the files in your project and watching the browser reload. Open the `./www/templates/tab-dash.thml` file and change the:

```
<h1>Dash</h1>
```

to:

```
<h1>Trencicity</h1>
```

The browser will refresh and you will see your changes immediately.

IONIC LAB

When you develop a mobile application for both iOS and Android, it helps to see what they will look like on both platforms. A quick way for you to see these differences is by using Ionic Lab. To do that, you just need to start up the server and pass a parameter like this:

```
$ ionic serve --lab
```

The results will look like the screenshot below. Notice how the tabs on iOS are at the bottom and the tabs on Android are at the top. Also, notice how the title on iOS displays in the center and the title on Android displays on the left.

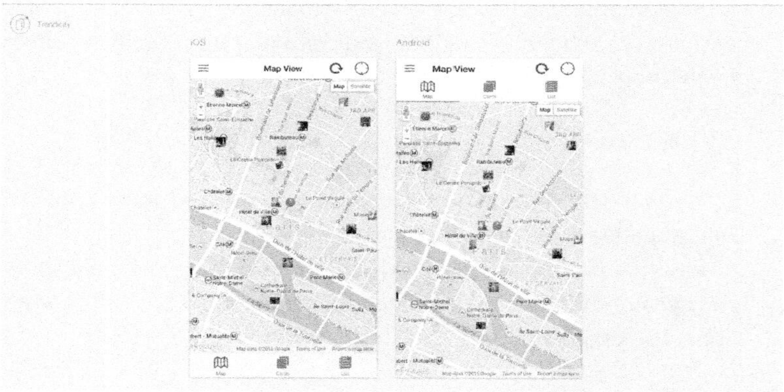

Ionic is actually applying `.platform-ios` and `.platform-android` classes to the UI components to display them in the browser. When deploying on a device, a Cordova hook will apply the appropriate class based on the platform.

Users of these platforms come to expect certain aspects of applications to appear the same. Ionic tries to adhere to these platform preferences. However, if you would like for your application to appear the same regardless of the platform, you can change this behavior quite easily on a feature by feature basis using the `$ionicConfigProvider`. For example, if you wanted the tabs to always show up at the bottom, regardless of the platform, you could change that. Likewise, if you wanted the navigation bar title to always be displayed in the center, you could change that as well. Below is an example of how you can make these changes by placing a `.config` block in your `app.js` file.

```
.config(function($ionicConfigProvider) {
  // Make tabs always show up at the bottom
  $ionicConfigProvider.tabs.position('bottom');
  // Align the navBar title to the center
  $ionicConfigProvider.navBar.alignTitle('center');
});
```

PROXIES

If your application needs to access APIs that do not allow Cross Origin Resource Sharing (CORS), you will encounter errors during browser testing. Fortunately, the Ionic team has built in the ability for you to proxy these requests through Ionic.

Open the ionic.project file in the root of your application.

```
{
    "name": "your_apps_name",
    "app_id": ""
}
```

Add a proxies array to your file:

```
{
    "name": "your_apps_name",
    "app_id": "",
    "proxies": [
        {
            "path": "/proxied/resources",
            "proxyUrl": "https://api.somesite.com/resources"
        }
    ]
}
```

In this example the `path` is the local path that you want to proxy and the `proxyUrl` is the actual API that you want that path to proxy the request to. In your application, you would now make requests in development mode to **http://localhost:8100/proxied/resources**, as opposed to **https://api.somesite.com/resources**.

It is important to note that this proxying is only necessary for testing in the browser. It will not be used when testing on a device, or through emulation.

Adding a platform

Before you can publish, or even build your application, you will need to decide which platforms you want to deploy onto. You then must tell Ionic, via the CLI, to install any necessary prerequisites for building for that platform. Let's add the iOS platform:

```
$ ionic platform ios
```

This will install any required dependencies and prepare your project for being built for the iOS platform. Note that you cannot add the iOS platform if you are not on an Apple computer.

Alternatively, you can add the Android platform as follows:

```
$ ionic platform android
```

The Android platform requires some additional setup as opposed to the iOS platform when on an Apple computer. You will read more about the Android setup later in this chapter.

If you do choose to test on the Android platform, it is suggested that you not use the default Android emulator. A common complaint about the emulator is that it is quite slow. Instead, you should install and use the Genymotion emulator, which is significantly faster than the default Android emulator. You can learn more about this emulator here: **www.genymotion.com/**

Creating a build

Creating a build is easy with Ionic. Create a build for the iOS platform with the following command:

```
$ ionic build ios
```

Once successfully built, you should see the following output:

```
** BUILD SUCCEEDED **
```

Running your build on an emulator

Ionic supports launching device emulators directly from the CLI. Launch your build in the iOS emulator (make sure you have ios-sim installed).

```
$ ionic emulate ios
```

If you skip the previous build step, Ionic creates the iOS platform build for you. After running this command, the iOS emulator will launch, and your application will appear in it.

Similarly to testing in the browser, you can make it so that the emulator will automatically refresh your application when you make changes to your project files. Run the following command, wait for the emulator to load your application, then make a change to one of your project files to see this:

```
$ ionic emulate ios -livereload
```

This can be a huge time saver versus having to build and launch the emulator each time you make some changes to your project.

Running on a device

Emulators are great, but you will want to test your application out on an actual device before you publish it.

IOS

To do this for iOS requires that you have an iOS developer account, and XCode running on an Apple device. Getting an iOS developer account is not free. You can learn more about it here: **developer.apple.com/programs/ios/**.

You can find the download for Xcode here: **developer.apple.com/xcode/downloads/**.

Once you have your account, and XCode is setup correctly, open the /platform/ios directory from your project in XCode, and then do your testing from XCode.

ANDROID

Up to this point we have primarily focused on building, emulating, and running iOS applications. That is because if you are developing on an Apple computer, it is the easiest and fastest environment to get up and running, but it avoids one of the great things about using Ionic. You write your application once, and can build it for both platforms! Let's take a moment to explore options for getting up and running on the Android platform.

ANDROID SDK LOCAL INSTALLATION

The first method of doing this is to download and install the Android SDK. The Android SDK can be found here: **developer.android.com/sdk/**. Steps to install it can be found here: **developer.android.com/sdk/installing/**.

IONIC BOX

Many people have found that installing the Android SDK can be difficult. Because of this, the Ionic team has created a Vagrant box to help ease the process. If you are unfamiliar with Vagrant, it is a platform for creating virtual machines to serve as development environments. You can learn more about it here: **www.vagrantup.com/**. It can work with many different VM providers, but the most common is VirtualBox.

In order to use the Vagrant box, you must first install VirtualBox, or another provider supported by Vagrant. VirtualBox is free and can be found here: **www.virtualbox.org/wiki/Downloads**. Once VirtualBox is installed, download and install Vagrant here: **www.vagrantup.com/downloads.html**.

Once you have both VirtualBox and Vagrant installed, move to the directory beneath your project, clone the Ionic box repo, and start it up.

```
$ cd ..
$ git clone https://github.com/driftyco/ionic-box
$ cd ionic-box
$ vagrant up
```

The first time you do this, it may take a couple of minutes since Vagrant needs to download the virtual machine image to use. Before you can start creating builds of your application on the Ionic box, you need to share your project code directory with the vm. Open the ionic-box/Vagrantfile in your editor of choice. Find the line:

```
# config.vm.synced_folder "../data", "/vagrant_data"
```

Change it to:

```
config.vm.synced_folder "../trendicity", "/home/vagrant/
trendicity"
```

Save the file and then reload your Vagrant instance:

```
$ vagrant reload
```

Now let's SSH into the Vagrant instance and create that Android build:

```
$ vagrant ssh
vagrant@ionic-android:~$ cd trendicity/
vagrant@ionic-android:~/trendicity$ ionic platform android
```

Now connect your Android device to your computer via USB. You can confirm that the device shows up on the Ionic box using the command:

```
vagrant@ionic-android:~/trendicity$ sudo /home/vagrant/
android-sdk-linux/platform-tools/adb devices
```

Confirm that your device is present, and then start the application on your device using the following command:

```
vagrant@ionic-android:~/trendicity$ ionic run android
```

You'll know it works when you see this message:

```
Installing app on device...
Launching application...
LAUNCH SUCCESS
```

Congratulations! You are now running your application on an actual Android device.

It may seem like this is a lot of trouble to go through just to get your application running on your device, but it is a testament to both how difficult the Android SDK setup is, and how dedicated the Ionic team is to making their suite of tools and services easy to use.

Adding plugins

Ionic and Cordova are powerful tools, but in order to improve performance and minimize the size of your application, they do not include everything you might want in the default installations. You can add additional features to your application by adding plugins. Let's add the geolocation plugin to our application in anticipation of using some geolocation features down the line in the Trendicity application.

From the root of your project, type the following command. Note that you can run this command either on your local machine, or on the Ionic box discussed above.

```
$ ionic plugin add org.apache.cordova.geolocation
```

Ionic will install the necessary components to allow you to use the geolocation features. That's all you need to do. You'll see how this plugin is used later on in this book when you dive into the details of the example Trendicity application.

You can explore the other plugins that are available here: **plugins.cordova.io/**.

Generate icons and splash screen

Prior to deploying your application to production, you will need to generate icons and a splash screen. Ionic is able to help you tremendously with this laborious process. What you need to do is create a resource directory under your project's root. Then place Photoshop (.psd), Illustrator (.ai) or .png files there. One for the icon named icon.png (for example) and one named splash.png (for example). Then you just need to run the command below and let Ionic take care of the cropping and resizing of the images. Ionic will even add the necessary entries for them in the `config.xml` file.

```
$ ionic resources
```

If you only want to generate an icon or you only want to generate a splash screen; you can just pass additional flags like this:

```
$ ionic resources --icon
$ ionic resources --splash
```

Source control best practices

Because Ionic and Cordova install numerous files that are specific to different platforms, it is not necessary to store many of them in your source control repository. Let's look through the project and see what should be stored in source control, and what should not.

Git and templated applications

If you are using Git (which the authors of this book highly recommend), and have created your application from the Ionic start command, you may notice that it has created a `.gitignore` file for you that already includes references to a number of directories that should be excluded from your repository. You can skip the rest of this section by choosing to review your `.gitignore` file, shown here:

```
$ cat .gitignore
# Specifies intentionally untracked files to ignore when
using Git
# http://git-scm.com/docs/gitignore

node_modules/
platforms/
plugins/
```

Root files

All of the files in the root directory should be stored in your source control repository. They contain configuration information about your project and without them you may not be able to build your application correctly.

Included directories

`./hooks`, `./scss`, and most importantly `./www` should all be stored in your source repository.

Excluded directories

`./node_modules`, `./platforms`, and `./plugins` should all be excluded from your source control repository. They contain numerous binary files and in addition contain builds of your application that will be constantly changing as you develop. They can also all be generated again when you check out your code on a new machine.

Summary

You are now ready to start building out your application. You have all of the tools you need at your disposal: you can test locally via the browser or an emulator, you can add plugins to access advanced features, and you can run your application on a real device.

Trendicity 3

Now that you have some more tools in your toolbelt, let's talk about developing an actual mobile application. Instagram is a very popular photo sharing application. To make these photos even more interesting and to show off some Ionic features, we will be referencing an application that we developed, called Trendicity. This application fetches and displays Instagram photos in a variety of ways.

One of the ways we display photos is by presenting their location on a map. Another is to display them in the form of *Tinder-Like Swipe* cards, where the user can indicate whether they like them or not. Lastly, we display them in a list view with a few more details.

The complete **Trendicity** application can be found on Github for your reference. You can download it and execute the application on your desktop browser, or you can deploy it to a device or simulator.

The Trendicity application is built as a side menu application, however, it also incorporates the use of tabs. We will discuss several aspects of the application. The *Side Menu* and the options the user can take, the *Search* feature, and the use of a *Loading Service* and the (*Map View*, *Card View* and *List View*) tabs.

Hang on to your hats as we dive into the code and take a bit of a roller coaster ride through the building of the application.

Side menu

The side menu consists of the following menu options:

- Home
- Favorites
- About
- Login/Logout

Below is a screenshot of the Trendicity side menu on a mobile device. For details on how to implement a side menu and the routes that go along with it, see Chapter 4: Implementing a side menu and setting up the routes.

Home

The *Home* menu option will invoke the `HomeCtrl` and display the *Map View Tab*. Here the map will display with the posts that are near the user's current location.

Favorites

The favorites section of the Trendicity app is split into three main parts: `FavoritesService`, `FavoritesCtrl` and the `favorites.html` template.

There are two types of favorites that can be stored: user-generated and post-related. The former is created using the `add-favorite` modal, while the latter is automatically linked to an Instagram post that contains a geolocation associated with it.

In this section we will examine how the favorites view is implemented and take a glimpse at the interactions that happen between `FavoritesCtrl` and `FavoritesService` in order to simplify the creation and deletion of favorites.

FAVORITES LIST

The favorites view displays existing favorites in a list. When the user enters the view, the favorites are automatically updated after the `$ionicView.enter` event fires:

```
$scope.$on('$ionicView.enter', function() {
    // Update favorites
    $scope.favorites = FavoritesService.getFavorites();
    ...
});
```

Each list item links to the map tab view and centers on the favorite's location. The following is the markup used to display the list of favorites:

```
<ion-list>
    <ion-item
      class="item-icon-right"
      ng-repeat="favorite in favorites track by favorite.id"
      ui-sref="app.home.map({ latitude: favorite.lat,
                              longitude: favorite.lng })">
      {{ favorite.city }}
      <i class="icon ion-ios-arrow-forward icon-
accessory"></i>
      <ion-option-button class="button-assertive"
                         ng-click="deleteFavorite(favorite)">
        Remove
      </ion-option-button>
    </ion-item>
</ion-list>
```

As an added bonus, we added a message that gets displayed if the user has not favorited anything.

```
<div class="vertical-center-container"
     ng-show="!favorites.length">
    <div class="vertical-center text-center">
      <h1><i class="icon ion-heart-broken assertive"></i></
h1>
      <p>Looks like you haven't favorited anything yet...</p>
    </div>
</div>
```

ADDING FAVORITES

In order to keep code maintainable, we decided to decouple the various components required to handle the creation of favorites. As a result, the `FavoritesCtrl`, `FavoritesService`, `add-favorite.html` template, along with the `add-favorite-form` directive work in tandem.

Clicking the “+” button located at the top-right corner of the favorites view triggers the opening of the `add-favorite` modal.

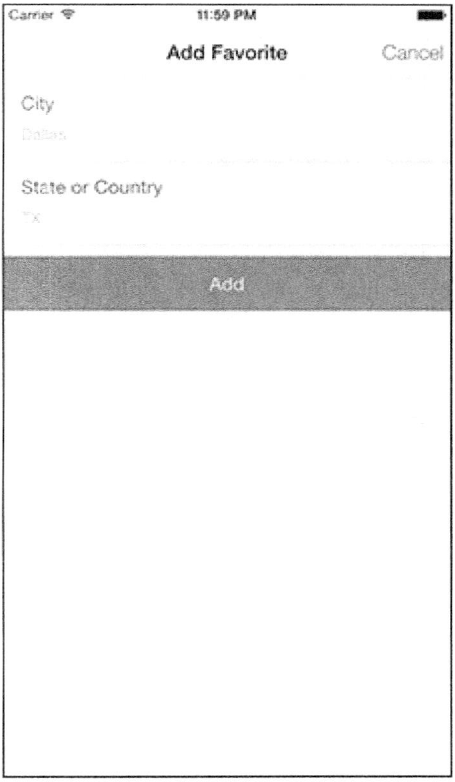


```
<ion-nav-buttons side="right">
    <button class="button button-icon ion-ios-plus-empty"
            ng-click="showModalAddFavorite()"></button>
</ion-nav-buttons>
```

The button triggers the `FavoriteCtrl`'s `showModalAddFavorite()` function, which in turn shows the preloaded `add-favorite` modal.

```
$scope.showModalAddFavorite = function () {
    $scope.modalAddFavorite.show();
};
```

The modal's content consists solely of the `add-favorite-form` directive.

```
<ion-content>
    <add-favorite-form on-submit="addFavorite(favorite)">
    </add-favorite-form>
</ion-content>
```

The `addFavoriteForm` directive takes in an `onSubmit()` function that gets passed to its inner scope. Once the form's inputs are all validated, the directive will call the function passed into its `on-submit` attribute.

Now, how does the directive know where to find the `addFavorite(favorite)` function? Recall that when we initialized the `add-favorite` modal we passed the `FavoriteCtrl`'s scope. Hence, the modal's scope inherits from its parent: the favorite view's controller.

```
// Create the add favorite modal that we will use later
$ionicModal
    .fromTemplateUrl('templates/modals/add-favorite.html', {
        scope: $scope
    }).then(function(modal) {
        $scope.modalAddFavorite = modal;
    });
```

The `addFavorite()` function has been attached to the controller's scope like so:

```
// Add a new favorite using the service
$scope.addFavorite = function(favorite) {
    FavoritesService.add(favorite).then(function () {
      $scope.favorites = FavoritesService.getFavorites();
      $scope.hideModalAddFavorite();
    });
};
```

After calling the `FavoritesService`'s `add()` function, it goes about updating the view's list of favorites and proceeds with hiding the active `add-favorite` modal.

ADD FAVORITE FORM DIRECTIVE

The `addFavoriteForm` directive uses `templates/directives/add-favorite-form.html` as its template. This view solely contains the form with basic AngularJS validation:

```
<form name="formAddFavorite" no-validate>
  <label class="item item-input item-stacked-label"
         ng-class="{ 'item-error': formAddFavorite.$attempt
&&
             formAddFavorite.city.$invalid, 'item-valid':
             formAddFavorite.city.$valid }">
    <span class="input-label">City</span>
    <input type="text" name="city" ng-model="favorite.city"
           placeholder="Dallas" required="required">
  </label>
  <label class="item item-input item-stacked-label"
         ng-class="{ 'item-error': formAddFavorite.$attempt
&&
             formAddFavorite.region.$invalid, 'item-valid':
             formAddFavorite.region.$valid }">
    <span class="input-label">State or Country</span>
    <input type="text" name="region" ng-
model="favorite.region"
           placeholder="TX" required="required">
  </label>
  <button class="button button-full button-positive"
          type="button" ng-click="submit()">Add</button>
</form>
```

The “Add” button calls the directive’s `submit()` function, which appends an `$attempt` property to the form, indicating that the user has submitted the form at least once. This property is used to highlight inputs that are not valid and which haven’t been modified yet.

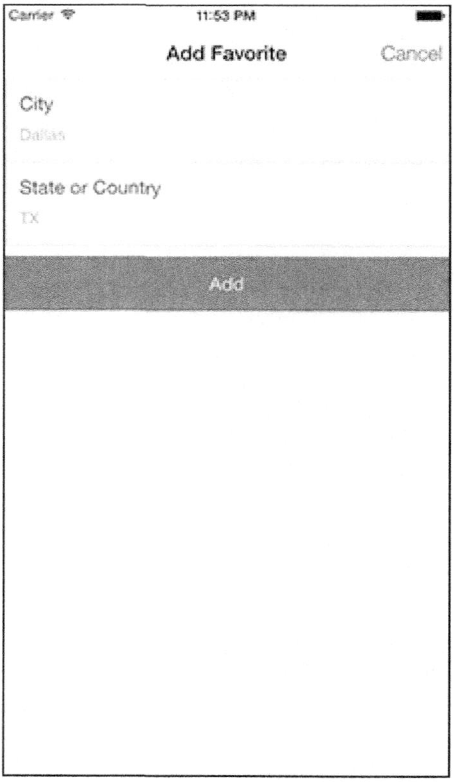

Finally, once the form is valid, the directive calls the `onSubmit()` function as can be seen here:

```
$scope.submit = function() {
    $scope.formAddFavorite.$attempt = true;

    if ($scope.formAddFavorite.$valid) {
      $scope.onSubmit({ favorite: $scope.favorite });
    }
};
```

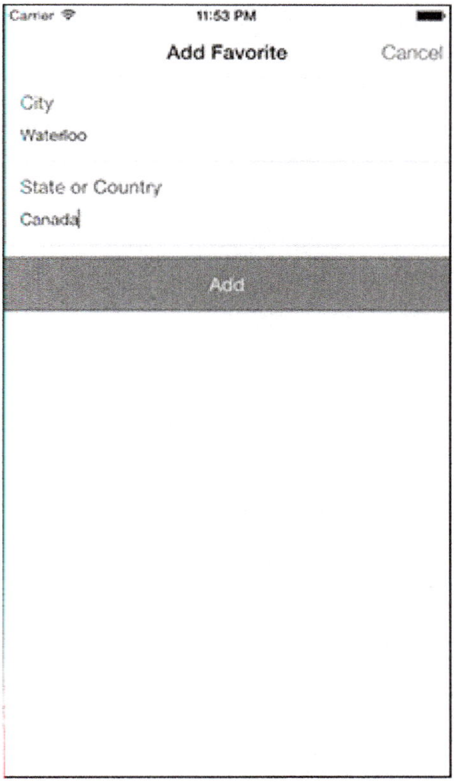

Furthermore, the form automatically clears its content whenever the parent modal is hidden. Attaching the following even handler to the `modal.hidden` event produces the desired effect:

```
$scope.$on('modal.hidden', function() {
    // Clear form
    $scope.favorite = null;
    $scope.formAddFavorite.$attempt = false;
    $scope.formAddFavorite.$setPristine(true);
});
```

REMOVING FAVORITES

Favorites can be removed by sliding the favorite item to the left, revealing the "Remove" button.

Clicking on the remove button calls the `FavoritesCtrl`'s `deleteFavorite()` function passing the currently referenced favorite. On the controller side, this function lets the `FavoritesService` handle the removal and finally updates the list of favorites:

```
$scope.deleteFavorite = function (favorite) {
    $scope.favorites = FavoritesService.delete(favorite);
};
```

FAVORITES SERVICE

The `FavoritesService` is the standardized way Trendicity keeps track of favorites. This approach allows us to maintain all of the favorites logic separated from the rest of the application. Moreover, creating a dedicated `FavoritesService` makes it available to any controller that requires it. As we will see later in this chapter, the FavoritesService is used in the list view tab to store favorited Instagram post locations.

The service provides three functions: add(), getFavorites() and delete().

As the name states, getFavorites() simply returns all stored favorites in local storage.

Adding favorites is handled differently depending on the type of favorite. For user-generated favorites, a city and region is included with the favorite data. These fields are used to determine the geolocation of the favorite using the GeolocationService's addressToPosition() function. The implementation of the latter function will be discussed in further detail in the following chapter. After having retrieved the proper latitude and longitude coordinates associated to the address, the favorite's format is standardized and stored by pushing to the local storage's favorites array.

```
var address = favorite.city + ', ' + favorite.region;
return GeolocationService.addressToPosition(address)
    .then(function (data) {
        var newLocation = {
          id: favoritesId,
          city: address,
          lat: data.latitude,
          lng: data.longitude
        };
        favorites.push(newLocation);
        localStorageService.set('Favorites', favorites);
    });
```

For post-specific favorites, the favorite is properly formatted within the list view's controller and, similarly to user favorites, pushed to the local storage's favorites array.

```
var newLocation = {
    id: favoritesId,
    city: favorite.city,
    lat: favorite.lat,
    lng: favorite.lng
};
favorites.push(newLocation);
localStorageService.set('Favorites', favorites);
```

In order to ensure proper tracking of favorites, the service generates ids for each new favorite. Each id is generated based on the current system date and time like so: `var favoritesId = new Date().getTime();`.

```
this.add = function(favorite) {
  var favorites = this.getFavorites() || [];
  var favoritesId = new Date().getTime();
  ...
};
```

Deleting favorites works by using lodash's `remove()` function. After having removed the passed favorite from the array of favorites, the function updates the appropriate local storage value and returns the modified array.

```
this.delete = function (favorite) {
    var favorites = this.getFavorites();
    _.remove(favorites, favorite);
    localStorageService.set('Favorites', favorites);
    return this.getFavorites();
};
```

About

The *About* menu option will display a slide box containing introductory information about the application. The first time the application is launched, the user will be presented with this page. This functionality is achieved using the `$ionicSlideBoxDelegate`, `ion-slide-box` and `ion-slide' components. If you are interested in the details of how this is implemented, take a look at the`IntroCtrl`in the`www/js/controllers/intro.js`file and the template in the`www/templates/intro.html` file.

Carrier
9:17 AM
Skip
Next
Welcome to Trendicity
Explore nearby Instagram posts on a map.
View nearby or trending posts as cards or in a list.
Login to see your feed and liked posts.

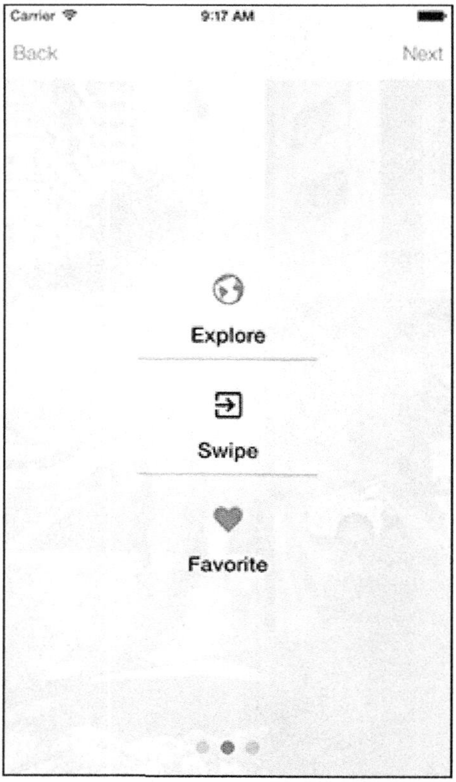
Carrier
9:17 AM
Back
Next
Explore
Swipe
Favorite

Login/Logout

The menu option for *Login* will be displayed if the user is not currently logged in. Once the user is logged in, the *Logout* menu option will be displayed.

The following is a snippet from the `www/templates/menu.html` file showing how this can be acheived using `ng-show()` and `ng-hide`.

```
<ion-item menu-close class="item-icon-left"
          ng-click="login()"
          ng-hide="isLoggedIn()">
  <i class="icon ion-log-in"></i>
  Login
</ion-item>
```

```
<ion-item menu-close class="item-icon-left"
          ng-click="logout()"
          ng-show="isLoggedIn()">
  <i class="icon ion-log-out"></i>
  Logout
</ion-item>
```

The `isLoggedIn()`, `login()` and `logout()` functions can be found in the `www/controllers/app.js file`.

```
// Determine if the user is logged into Instagram
$scope.isLoggedIn = function() {
  return InstagramService.isLoggedIn();
};

// Open the login modal
$scope.login = function() {
  $scope.loginModal.show();
};

// Log the user out when they invoke the logout link
$scope.logout = function() {
  InstagramService.logout();
};
```

The `isLoggedIn()` function is going to ask the `InstagramService` if the user is logged in. The `logout()` function is going to ask the `InstagramService` to log the user out. We will talk more about the `InstagramService` in Chapter 8.

In order to do more interesting things with Instagram, we need the user to login to Instagram. To achieve this, we are going to make use of an `$ionicModal` to give a brief description of what we intend to do if the user chooses to proceed. Upon selecting the *Login* menu option, the `login()` function will be invoked, and the user will be presented with the following login modal.

```
// Create the login modal that we will use later
$ionicModal.fromTemplateUrl('templates/login.html', {
  scope: $scope,
  animation: 'slide-in-up'
}).then(function(modal) {
  $scope.loginModal = modal;
});

//Cleanup the modal when we're done with it!
$scope.$on('$destroy', function() {
  $scope.loginModal.remove();
});
```

Instead of displaying a traditional login modal, we are going to inform the user of what we are intending to do, and what they can expect to be able to do once they login to Instagram. Once the user confirms that they want to login to Instagram, we are going to invoke the `loginToInstagram()` function in `www/controllers/app.js`.

```
// Perform the OAuth login to Instagram
$scope.loginToInstagram = function() {
  $scope.loginModal.hide();
  InstagramService.login();
};
```

This function will perform OAuth level authentation using the InAppBrowser Cordova plugin. We are using this plugin to open a window with the external Instagram login URL. The Trendicity application is not processing the username and password.

Search

The *Search* icon is represented by a magnifying glass in the top right portion of the *Card* and *List* views. The user has the following search options:

- Trending - "popular" posts currently trending on Instagram.
- Nearby - posts within a 1K mile radius of the user's current location.
- My Feed - Instagram feed for the logged in user.
- My Liked Posts - posts that the logged in user has liked.

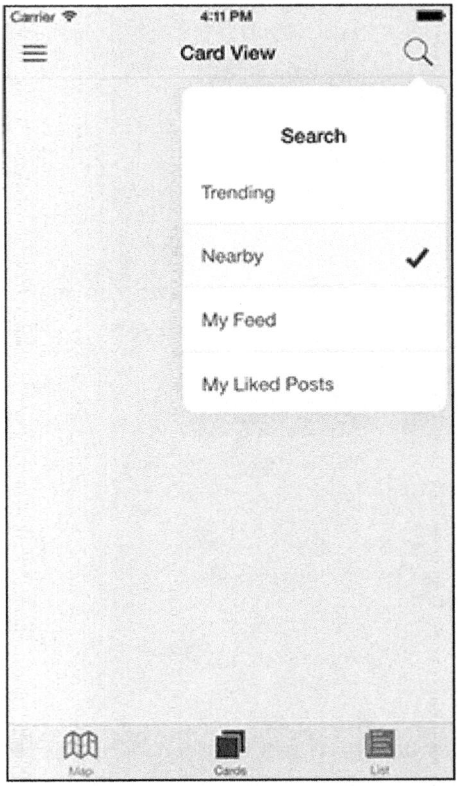

In the `HomeCtrl`, we setup the search functionality. The code below has been slightly abbreviated in order to focus on the search feature.

First, we set up a couple of scope variables to hold the posts and the search value. We are using a JavaScript object for both so that the bindings on them will not get lost when the values are changed.

```
  $scope.model =  PostsService.getModel();
  $scope.search = { value: POST_TYPE.NEARBY};
```

Next, we setup the `$scope.getPosts()` function that will be responsible for determining which function needs to be called based on the search value.

```
$scope.getPosts = function(value) {
  if (value === POST_TYPE.TRENDING) {
    PostsService.findPopularPosts();
  } else if (value === POST_TYPE.NEARBY) {
    $scope.findNearbyPosts();
  } else if (value === POST_TYPE.USER_FEED) {
    PostsService.findUserFeedPosts();
  } else if (value === POST_TYPE.LIKED) {
    PostsService.findLikedPosts();
  }
};
```

By setting up a `$watch` on the search value, we can have the `$scope.getPosts()` function invoked when the search value is changed in the `ionicPopover` component.

```
$scope.$watch('search.value', function(newValue) {
    // Triggered when user changes search value
    $scope.updatePosts(newValue);
});

$scope.updatePosts = function (searchValue) {
  $scope.getPosts(searchValue);
  $scope.closePopover();
  $ionicScrollDelegate.scrollTop();
};
```

To implement the `ionicPopover`, we first need to load up the HTML for it by calling the `fromTemplateUrl()` function. Here we set the scope for it to be the same scope that we are using in the `HomeCtlr`. When the template is loaded, we set the popover in our scope variable so that we can reference it later.

```
$ionicPopover.fromTemplateUrl('templates/search.html', {
  scope: $scope,
}).then(function(popover) {
  $scope.popover = popover;
});
```

Below is a snippet of the `search.html` template. Here we are using the `ion-popover-view` component to define the view. We use the `ion-header-bar` component to display the title for the popover. We use the `ion-content` component to wrap the `ion-radio` components. The `ion-radio` components will be responsible for setting the appropriate search value when selected.

```
<ion-popover-view>
   <ion-header-bar>
     <h1 class="title">Search</h1>
   </ion-header-bar>
   <ion-content>
     <ion-radio ng-model="search.value" value="TR">
       Trending
     </ion-radio>
     <ion-radio ng-model="search.value" value="NB">
       Nearby
     </ion-radio>
     <ion-radio ng-model="search.value" value="UF">
       My Feed
     </ion-radio>
     <ion-radio ng-model="search.value" value="LP">
       My Liked Posts
     </ion-radio>
   </ion-content>
</ion-popover-view>
```

The `ionicPopover` will be displayed when the user selects the Nav button, which is defined in `templates/home.html`. Below is a snippet from that file.

```
<ion-nav-buttons side="right">
  <button class="button button-icon icon ion-ios-search"
          ng-click="openPopover($event)"></button>
</ion-nav-buttons>
```

When the user touchs the *Search* magnifiying glass icon, the `openPopover()` function will be invoked. All we have to do then is just ask the popover to show itself. When a selection is made, the `closePopover` function will be invoked. In that function, we just make sure that the popover is defined and `isShown()`. If so, we ask it to hide itself. The last thing we need to do is to set up a `$destroy` listener so that the popover is removed from the DOM when the scope is destroyed.

```
$scope.openPopover = function($event) {
  $scope.popover.show($event);
};

$scope.closePopover = function() {
  if ($scope.popover && $scope.popover.isShown()) {
    $scope.popover.hide();
  }
};

// Cleanup the popover when we're done with it!
$scope.$on('$destroy', function() {
  if ($scope.popover) {
    $scope.popover.remove();
  }
});
```

Loading service

When photos are loading, instead of the user wondering what the application is doing, we would like to inform the user that we are loading data. We can make use of the `$ionicLoading` component to achieve this.

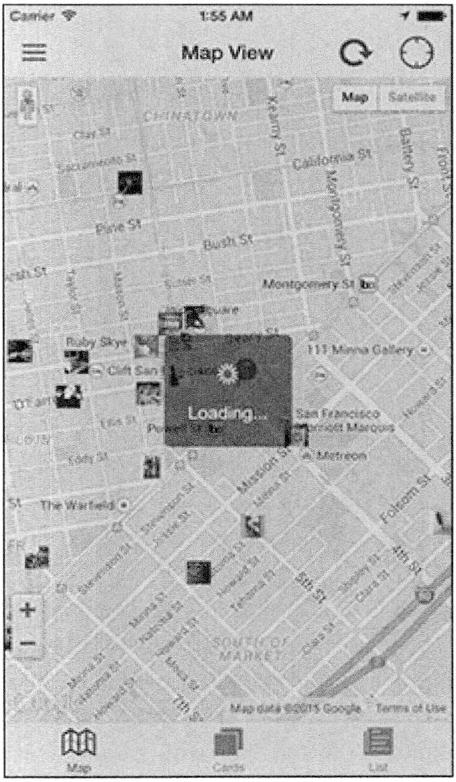

A clever way to use the `$ionicLoading` component is to place it inside of an HTTP interceptor. We have slighlty abbreviated the Trendicity code below so that we can focus on this particular topic.

```
.factory('TrendicityInterceptor',
  function ($injector, $q) {

    var hideLoadingModalIfNecessary = function() {
      var $http = $http || $injector.get('$http');
      if ($http.pendingRequests.length === 0) {
        $injector.get('$ionicLoading').hide();
      }
    };

    return {
      request: function(config) {
        $injector.get('$ionicLoading').show();
```

```
        },
        requestError: function(rejection) {
          hideLoadingModalIfNecessary();
          return $q.reject(rejection);
        },
        response: function(response) {
          hideLoadingModalIfNecessary();
          return response;
        },
        responseError: function(rejection) {
          hideLoadingModalIfNecessary();
          return $q.reject(rejection);
        }
      };
    }
  );
```

The `request()` function will be invoked when an HTTP request is made. Here we show the "Loading" message. To avoid a circular dependency error, we need to use the Angular `$injector` component to obtain the `$ionicLoading` service.

The `requestError()` function will be invoked when an HTTP request error occurs. Here we will call the `hideLoadingModalIfNecessary()` function, which will check to see if there are any pending HTTP requests. If not, the `ionicLoading` service will be be asked to hide itself.

The `response()` function will be invoked when a succuessful HTTP response is received. Here we do the same thing we did in the `requestError` function.

The `responseError()` function will be invoked when an HTTP response error occurs. Again, we do the same thing we did in the `response` and `requestError` functions.

In order to get our HTTP interceptor to work, we need to essentially let AngularJS know about it. Generally, this is done in the `www/app.js` file as follows. Here we are adding our intercepter to the array of interceptors on the `$httpProvider`.

```
.config(function($httpProvider) {
   $httpProvider.interceptors.push('TrendicityInterceptor');
});
```

Notice we didn't provide the actual message when we asked the `ionicLoading` componet to show itself. The reason for that is because we have configured the default message in the `www/app.js` file.

```
.constant('$ionicLoadingConfig', {
  template:
    '<h3>
       <icon ios="ion-loading-d"
             android="ion-loading-c"
            default="ion-refreshing">
        </icon>
      </h3>Loading...'
})
```

We will go over this template in more detail in Chapter 7: Designing the application. For now, we just wanted to show you why we didn't need to pass in the message to the `ionicLoading` show function.

Map view tab

The map view tab will display the current result set of posts on an interactive map. A marker will be displayed to denote the user's current location. Markers will also be displayed to represent the location of where the photo was taken. When a post marker is touched, the associated photo will be displayed. If you pan around in the map and then invoke the *Refresh* icon in the upper right corner; this will load posts for that location on the map. You can also choose the *Current Location* icon in the upper right corner; this will take you back to your current location. For details as to how the map view is implemented, see Chapter 5: Integrating a map view with Ionic.

Card view tab

The card view tab will display the photos as a deck of cards stacked on top of each other. The user can drag or swipe a card to the left to unlike the photo. Likewise, the user can drag or swipe a card to the right to like the photo.

These cards in this view are very much like the cards seen in the popular *Tinder* mobile application. This type of functionality has commonly been referred to as *Tinder Cards*.

Max Lynch, one of the co-founders of Drifty (the company responsible for bringing us Ionic) has created a library that allows us to create *Tinder Cards* in our mobile application. This type of add-on library is commonly referred to as an *ion* by the Ionic team. They typically showcase ways to use Ionic to do even more exciting things.

This library uses CSS animation to achieve the angling of the cards as they are swiped or dragged across the screen. It also uses a new physics-style animation library **Collide** to implement a spring-like effect when you pull a card straight down.

Prior to the `ionic-contrib-tinder-cards` library, a very similar ion called `ionic-ion-swipe-cards` was created. The `ionic-ion-swipe-cards` ion is based on apps like **Jelly**. The main difference between the `ionic-contrib-tinder-cards` and the `ionic-ion-swipe-cards` is the direction of the drag/swipe. Also, the `ionic-contrib-tinder-cards` has the "Nope/Like" feature as seen in the *Tinder* application. The Trendicity app is using the `ionic-contrib-tinder-cards` ion.

Working files

The files related to the card view functionality are located at: `www/templates/tab-card.html`,`www/templates/card-intro.html` and `www/js/controllers/card.js`.

Introductory popup

When navigating to the card view tab for the first time, we decided to display an explanatory popup message introducing the user and familiarizing them to our Tinder-Like card functionality.

We employ the `$ionicPopup` service to display an Ionic-styled popup message. The service allows you to define four types of popups:

- `show(options)`: Fully customizable popup with loads of options.
- `alert(options)`: Popup with a single button.
- `confirm(options)`: Displays a confirmation message with with "Cancel" and "OK" buttons.
- `prompt(options)`: Requires the user to interact with an input field and displays the same buttons from the `confirm` popup type.

For our Trendicity application, we define a custom popup like so:

```
$ionicPopup.show({
    title: 'Swipe Cards',
    templateUrl: 'templates/card-intro.html',
    scope: $scope,
    buttons: [
```

```
        {
            text: 'Next',
            type: 'button-positive',
            onTap: function(e) {
                if (slidebox.currentIndex() == 0) {
                    // Go to next slide
                    slidebox.next();

                    // Change button text
                    e.target.innerHTML = 'OK';

                    e.preventDefault();
                } else {
                    // Close popup
                    return;
                }
            }
        }
    ]
});
```

The popup's body is defined by either the `template` or `templateUrl` fields in the options object passed into the `show()` function. For Trendicity, since our template is a little complex, we defined it in its own file and linked it by specifying its location relative to the index: `templates/card-intro.html`.

Our template includes a slide box to allow for fluid transitions between one explanatory image to the other.

```
<ion-slide-box does-continue="false" show-pager="false"
               delegate-handle="card-intro-slidebox"
               ng-init="disableSlideBox()">
    <ion-slide>
        <img class="full-image" src="images/swipe-
right.png" />
    </ion-slide>
    <ion-slide>
        <img class="full-image" src="images/swipe-
left.png" />
    </ion-slide>
</ion-slide-box>
```

The slide box component comes with its own AngularJS service called `$ionicSlideBoxDelegate`. This service allows you to control the components's behavior, such as switching from slide to slide, controlling the state of the auto-play feature and disabling slides from sliding. The addition of an update() function, which explicitly triggers the rendering of the slide box, is handy when changing the number of slides dynamically and resizing the directive to adapt its size to fit new slide dimensions.

For our purposes, we opted for disabling any automatic sliding by setting the does-continue attribute to false and even disallowed the user from swiping the individual slides with the initial call to our controller's disableSlideBox() function which would disable all slides:

```
$scope.disableSlideBox = function() {
    $ionicSlideBoxDelegate.enableSlide(false);
};
```

This would simplify handling the flow of the tutorial popup by requiring all steps to pass through the buttons.

The onTap() function of Ionic's popup service let us provide custom logic for the popup's functionality. In essence, if the current slide being displayed was the first one, tapping on the "Next" button would switch to the following slide by invoking our slide box delegateInstance's' (given by $ionicSlideBoxDelegate.$getByHandle("card-intro-slidebox")) next() function and change the button's text to "OK" as well as preventing the popup from closing. Otherwise, meaning when on the second and final slide, we would simply call return, which would close the popup.

Finally, each time the user accesses the card view, we execute a simple check on the locally stored seenCardIntro value to determine if the user has to see the introduction or not.

Card view

In the www/templates/tab-card.html file, we setup a collection of cards using the td-cards element. This is a container that will hold our td-card elements. We use a ng-repeat to iterate over the posts. Then we define some attributes that allow us to respond to the user's interactions with the cards.

```
<ion-view title="Card View">
  <ion-content class="has-header padding" scroll="false">
    <td-cards>
      <td-card ng-repeat="post in model.currentPosts"
          on-destroy="cardDestroyed($index)"
          on-transition-left="cardTransitionedLeft($index)"
          on-transition-
```

```
right="cardTransitionedRight($index)">
          <div class="image">
            <div class="no-text">NOPE</div>
            <img ng-
src="{{ post.images.low_resolution.url }}" />
            <div class="yes-text">LIKE</div>
          </div>
        </td-card>
      </td-cards>
    </ion-content>
</ion-view>
```

Card view controller

We need the `CardViewCtrl` to disable the ability to slide the content, which would normally display the *Side Menu*. If we didn't disable this, it would conflict with our *Tinder* card functionality. Here we use the `$ionicSideMenuDelegate` to disable the drag event on the content upon entering the view. When leaving the view, we enable it so that the other views will be able to support the dragging of the content to open the side menu.

```
.controller('CardViewCtrl', function (
  $scope,
  $ionicSideMenuDelegate,
  $ionicPopup,
  $ionicSlideBoxDelegate,
  localStorageService) {

  // Disable side-menu drag so that it doesn't interfere
with our tinder cards functionality
  $scope.$on('$ionicView.enter', function() {
    $ionicHistory.clearHistory();
    $ionicSideMenuDelegate.canDragContent(false);
  });

  $scope.$on('$ionicView.leave', function() {
    $ionicSideMenuDelegate.canDragContent(true);
  });

  $scope.cardTransitionedLeft = function(index) {
    console.log('cardTransitionedLeft with index:' + index);
    if (!InstagramService.isLoggedIn()) {
      return;
    }
```

```
    var post = $scope.model.currentPosts[index];
    if (post.user_has_liked) {
      PostsService.dislikePost(post.id)
      .success(function() {
        console.log('you disliked it!');
      });
    } else {
      console.log('you didnt like it in the first place!');
    }
  };

  $scope.cardTransitionedRight = function(index) {
    console.log('cardTransitionedRight with index:' + index);

    var post = $scope.model.currentPosts[index];
    if (!post.user_has_liked) {
      PostsService.likePost(post.id)
      .success(function () {
        console.log('you liked it!');
      });
    } else {
      console.log('you already liked it previously!');
    }
  };

  $scope.cardDestroyed = function(index) {
    console.log('cardDestroyed with index:' + index);
    $scope.model.currentPosts.splice(index, 1);
  };
});
```

The `cardTransitionedLeft()` and `cardTransitionRight()` functions are basically the same except that the `cardTransitioned-Left()` function will remove a *like*, and the `cardTransitionRight()` function will add a *like*. Both will check to see if they even need to make a call to Instagram or not. However, if the user tries to *like* a card and they are not logged in, they will be prompted to login. Upon a successful login, the card will be liked. This is the result of our authentication solution. You can read more about how this is achieved by reading Chapter 6: Authentication.

The `cardDestroyed()` function will be called once a card has transitioned and has been destroyed. Here we just remove the card from the posts array.

List view tab

Trendicity's list view tab was developed in order to show off some of Ionic's core list functionality. Popular components such as pull-to-refresh, button bars, action sheets, and gestures are included in the view. In this section, we will explore the development process of working with lists, and the aforementioned components.

Related files

The files related to the list view functionality are located at: `www/templates/tab-list.html`, `www/js/controllers/list.js` and `www/js/directives/on-dbl-tap.js`. The routing has been configured in the `www/js/app.js` module like so:

```
.state('app.home.list', {
    url: '/list',
    views: {
        'tab-list' :{
            templateUrl: 'templates/tab-list.html',
            controller: 'ListViewCtrl'
        }
    }
})
```

Template layout

The list view template can be divided into three sections: the pull-to-refresh component, the list of posts, and the button bar containing accessible user-actionable buttons.

Refreshing the list of posts

Ionic provides a very useful directive aptly named `ion-refresher`. To implement this component, it is as easy as including the tag in your view's markup and attaching a function in the view's controller to handle your application's behavior once the user has finished pulling the content down and triggered the refreshing mechanism.

To keep it simple, we opted to use a custom refreshing icon instead of the default (`ion-arrow-down-c`) supplied within the directive and set some custom text to be displayed when pulling down on the list of posts.

```
<ion-refresher pulling-icon="ion-ios-arrow-up"
               spinner="none"
               pulling-text="Pull to refresh..."
               on-refresh="doRefresh()">
</ion-refresher>
```

Note that the directive allows you to override its default settings through the following attributes:

- `on-refresh`: Function to call once user has completely pulled the content down triggering the refresh mechanism.
- `on-pulling`: Function to call once user starts pulling the content down.

- `spinner`: Spinner to display once refreshing is in progress. Setting this attribute to none will remove both the spinner and the icon.
- `pulling-icon`: Ionicon to display when user is pulling down.
- `pulling-text`: Text to display when user is pulling down.
- `refreshing-icon`: Ionicon to display once the refresh mechanism has been triggered.
- `disable-pulling-rotation`: Stops rotation of icon once `on-refresh` is reached.

A noteworthy improvement to the `ion-refresher` component is the addition of a small timer, which causes the refresher to be displayed for a minimum of 400ms, for cases when your data is fetched in the blink of an eye. In these situations, the inclusion of a timeout creates the perception of a smoother refreshing process signalling to the user that data has been fetched properly.

Back to Trendicity, our refresher is setup to trigger our controller's `doRefresh()` function when expecting to fetch new posts. Below is the code to handle the refreshing mechanism.

```
$scope.doRefresh = function() {
    $scope.getPosts($scope.search.value);

    // Hide ion-refresher
    $scope.$broadcast('scroll.refreshComplete');
};
```

As explained in the previous sections, we make use of `HomeCtrl`'s `getPosts()` function, passing it the current search value. This allows the application to know what type of posts to target when fetching data from Instagram's API as determined by the currently selected type of feed in the search's popover list.

Lastly, we finish off by broadcasting the `scroll.refreshComplete` event to signal that directive's refreshing mechanism has finished, causing the `ion-refresher` to return to its initial state and become hidden.

List of posts

When working with large lists of items you have many ways of offloading the mobile device's limited hardware to maintain fluid application functionality. There is Ionic's `ion-infinite-scroll` directive, which loads new data in preset intervals defined by you. Another feature, `collection-repeat`, mimics other well known mobile platform list views such as iOS's `UITableViewController`, by only loading a few rows of list items at a time, removing the ones off the device's screen. By minimizing the number of DOM elements required to be added and display your list's content, `collection-repeat` significantly improves your application's performance.

Compared to other solutions, `collection-repeat` is an elegant directive that doesn't require any complicated setup to gain the potential performance boost. The only configuration required from the developer is to specify each item's height and width. This can be achieved by calling functions and optionally passing in the list item's index to determine each item's size. Otherwise, using a scoped variable or static value is also an acceptable approach.

In our case, we do not modify the item dimensions, however we perform a calculation based on the device's screen width to determine the constant item size. Therefore, we summed the heights of either screen width or Instagram image width (whichever is the smallest), as well as the heights of `item-avatar` and `button-bar`:

```
function getItemHeight() {
    var screenWidth = window.innerWidth,
        imageWidth = 640,
        itemAvatarHeight = 76,
        buttonBarHeight = 46;
    var min = (screenWidth < imageWidth) ? screenWidth :
imageWidth;
    return min + itemAvatarHeight + buttonBarHeight;
}

$scope.itemHeight = getItemHeight();
```

And in the template we use `collection-repeat` like so:

```
<div class="list-post"
     collection-repeat="post in model.currentPosts"
     collection-item-height="itemHeight">
    ...
</div>
```

Note that we haven't defined the `collection-item-width` attribute's value since it would have been equivalent to the directive's default value of `100%` in any case.

An important thing to note when working with the `collection-repeat` directive is the fact that it will apply absolute positioning on your list items, which may cause unexpected display behavior. To counter this, simply apply the following CSS rules to the list items:

```
left: 0;
right: 0;
```

In our application, we included this segment in our `list-post` CSS class.

With the release of the first candidate for version 1.0 of Ionic, an updated implementation of `collection-repeat` removes the need for specifying the dimensions of each item. The directive can automatically determine the proper size of the first element and will apply this same dimension to all other elements in the collection. Given that in our list of posts, each item has the same dimensions, we opted to let `collection-repeat` take care of dynamically assigning the item dimensions. As such, our `getItemHeight()` function was no longer necessary.

Liking posts

Similar to the card view, we have implemented a post liking mechanism in the list view. To spice things up, we decided to mimic Instagram's functionality by allowing the user to double tap the post's image as well as tapping the dedicated button to designate the liking of a post.

Implementing this functionality with a dedicated button is pretty straightforward. First of all, we use the `button-bar` class as a wrapper for the like and comment buttons:

```
<div class="button-bar bar-light">
    <button class="button"
            ng-click="like($index)"
            ng-class="{ 'button-assertive':
post.user_has_liked }">
            <i class="icon ion-heart"></i>
            {{ post.likes.count | number }}
    </button>
    <button class="button">
            <i class="icon ion-chatbubbles"></i>
            {{ post.comments.count | number }}
    </button>
</div>
```

Furthermore, we add a `ng-class` attribute that would apply the `button-assertive` class on the like button if the particular post has been liked. A simple `ng-click` sufficed for the purpose of invoking our controller's `like($index)` function.

For the image double tapping, we are going to introduce the topic of gestures. Conveniently, Ionic provides multiple directives for automatically handling common gestures such as tapping, dragging, and pressing, amongst numerous others. These gestures come from a popular framework called `HammerJS` that handles the actual gesture-recognition mechanism for Ionic and our application. Ionic's directive definitions do not include the double-tapping gesture we want to capture so we examined the source code responsible for all of the other gestures' directives, as well as determining the corresponding `HammerJS` gesture name. We then defined an equal solution for the double tap gesture:

```
.directive('onDblTap', function($ionicGesture, $parse) {
    return {
        restrict: 'A',
        link: function($scope, $element, $attr) {
            var fn = $parse($attr['onDblTap']);

            var listener = function(ev) {
                $scope.$apply(function() {
                    fn($scope, {
                        $event: ev
                    });
                });
            };

            var gesture = $ionicGesture.on('doubletap',
listener, $element);

            // Remove gesture recognition on DOM element
            $scope.$on('$destroy', function() {
                $ionicGesture.off(gesture, 'doubletap',
listener);
            });
        }
    };
});
```

In the template, the double tapping gesture directive is included like so:

```
<img ... on-dbl-tap="like($index)" ... />
```

However, with the newest release candidate for version 1 of Ionic, a `on-double-tap` has already been provided. The previous steps were required up until beta 14, but is no longer required if using the latest Ionic platform. Therefore, we opted to use the built-in `on-double-tap` directive for our posts which meant that our custom directive was no longer required.

When the user double taps the image within an interval of 250ms, the `like($index)` function is invoked passing the list item's index.

Here is our `like()` function's implementation:

```
$scope.like = function(index) {
    if (!InstagramService.isLoggedIn()) {
        // Show login modal
        $scope.loginModal.show();
        return;
```

```
    }

    var post = $scope.model.currentPosts[index];
    if (!post.user_has_liked) {
        InstagramService.likePost(post.id)
        .success(function () {
            console.log('you liked it!');

            // Update post to reflect like
            $scope.model.currentPosts[index].user_has_liked
= true;
            $scope.model.currentPosts[index].likes.count =
post.likes.count + 1;
        });
    } else {
        console.log('you already liked it previously!');
    }
};
```

Finally, the `like()` function either displays the login modal, or goes forth with liking the post using Instagram's API depending if the user is logged in or not.

Displaying options with action sheet

In tune with new advancements in mobile design, along with the advent of new components such as Android's hamburger menus and iOS's action sheets, Ionic has introduced its own implementation of this component aptly named: `$ionicActionSheet`. This service lets you invoke fully stylized action sheets from your controller, without having to add any markup whatsoever.

For our purposes, we want to allow the users to have more options when it comes to interacting with posts.

```
$scope.displayOptions = function(index) {
    // Get post
    var post = $scope.model.currentPosts[index];

    var buttons = [{ text: 'Like' }];

    // Add button if location available
    if (post.location !== null &&
        post.location.longitude !== null &&
        post.location.latitude !== null) {
        buttons.push({ text: 'Favorite Post\'s Location' });
    }

    var actionSheet = $ionicActionSheet.show({
        buttons: buttons,
```

```
            titleText: 'Options',
            cancelText: 'Close',
            buttonClicked: function(i) {
                if (i === 0) {
                    // Like post
                    $scope.like(index);
                } else if (i === 1) {
                    // Add post's location to favorites
                    FavoritesService.add({
                        city: (post.location.name
                            || post.user.username + '\'s post'),
                        lng: post.location.longitude,
                        lat: post.location.latitude
                    });

                    // Display confirmation
                    $ionicLoading.show({
                        template: 'Added to Favorites',
                        noBackdrop: true,
                        duration: 1000
                    });
                }

                // Close action sheet
                return true;
            }
        });
    };
```

First, we want to allow users to favorite the post's location for future revisiting. Therefore, we ensure that the particular post has a location field and has valid longitude and latitude coordinates. We then add a new button to the action sheet. The `buttonClicked()` function allows us to handle particular buttons based on their indexes in the `buttons` array. In order to close (hide) the action sheet, you are required to return `true` within the `buttonClicked()` function. An alternative way of achieving the same effect is to store the action sheet definition in a variable and then calling the `close()` function on itself.

Combined with the `hold` gesture, you get a pretty intuitive user interface. Naturally, we added the provided `on-hold` directive to trigger the action sheet whenever the user holds their finger on the post's image:

```
<img ... on-hold="displayOptions($index)"/>
```

The `$ionicActionSheet` service includes additional options that can be defined when invoking it, which we didn't bother modifying in our application, such as:

- `cancelOnStateChange`: Whether to close the action sheet when changing the state (route). Defaults to true.
- `destructiveText`: Text for a button separated from other options and highlighted with a `button-assertive` class. Used for actions that are irreversible.
- `destructiveButtonClicked`: Handler function for the destructive button.

A possible use case for the last two options would be to include a *flag* button, similar to what's found in Instagram's application.

Finally, since the release of Ionic's version 1 release candidate, action sheets defined using the `$ionicActionSheet` service follow the proper design guidelines in accordance with the different mobile platforms. As a result, these sheets look native on iOS and Android.

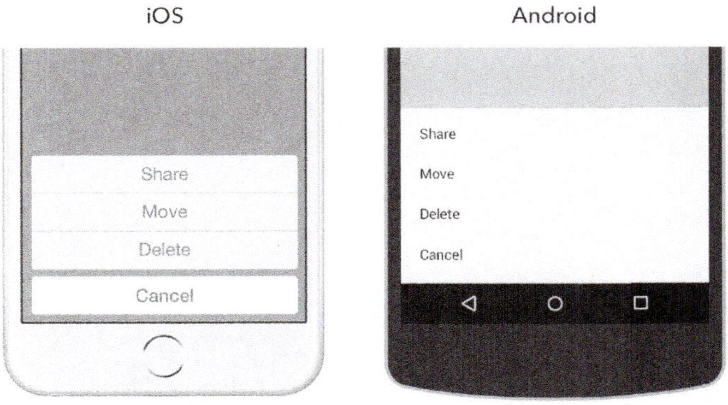

Summary

We have taken a long journey through most of the steps for building an Ionic application. Now you know how the Trendicity application was constructed, and how it works. Along the way you learned about Side Menu options, implementing a Search using ionicPopover, triggering the Loading Service, and the use of Tabs in an Ionic application. You learned how to use an ion-slide-box in the Card view intro. You were shown how simple it is to create Tinder cards in the the Card view. You also learned how to use ion-refresher, ionicActionSheet and collection-repeat in the List view. You are now well on your way to building your very own hybrid applications.

In the following chapter, we will examine how to fully implement a side menu, and how to set up the routes that go with it.

Designing the application 4

Design is an integral part of any modern mobile application. Ultimately, it defines the way users are to tap into your application's functionality. With recent advancements in design philosophy, through Apple's iOS 7 platform, Android Lollipop, and Google's Material Design, design is now at the forefront of how users engage with applications. Numerous frameworks have been built to give developers the toolsets and guidelines they need to enhance user experience while unleashing the full potential of their application's capabilities. In keeping in touch with the growing importance attributable to proper design principles, Ionic provides numerous tools in the form of components and icons with the intention of enriching the usability of developers' applications.

Before jumping into how Trendicity is designed, we will begin by exploring the tools offered by the Ionic SDK and how they can be applied in your applications to facilitate the design process.

Essentially, Ionic provides customizable building blocks in the form of layout components, built-in animations, a unique iconset called Ionicons, as well as multiple AngularJS directives and services. To top it all off, the SDK has been built with extensibility in mind, letting you easily adapt the behavior and look of the numerous precompiled assets through the use of Sass variables and mixins, saving you from the hassle of writing huge chunks of styling code.

Layout components

Ionic comes with a set of UI components that are great for handling the layout of your application. The fundamental utilities you will become accustomed to using when building mobile applications are: `ion-header`, `ion-content`, and `ion-list`. These AngularJS directives are components built by the Ionic team for your convenience and should be regarded as building blocks to quickly generate the basic implementation of your application's navigation, look, and feel. In their most basic states, the provided Ionic components are built on top of a robust collection of extensible CSS classes such as `bar`, `content`, and `list`. These CSS classes will become useful in the future when trying to create custom directives of your own or simply modifying the look and feel of certain user interface elements.

With its vast array of styling classes, Ionic lets you quickly use HTML tags you're used to working with, and make them look fit for mobile. An emphasis has been put onto the organization of your application's actionable elements, such as: buttons, lists, list items, forms, and input fields. With the inclusion of wrapper classes, notably `list`, `button-bar`, `card`, and `item`, Ionic can in essence take care of your components' arrangement.

A predefined set of general design utilities have been provided and encompass colors, spacing, and animations. In total, nine colors ranging from *assertive* to *energized* have been defined and can be found in `www/lib/ionic/scss/_variables.scss`, which comes as part of the Ionic source code. For your convenience, here is the full list of colors and their associated values:

```
$light:                         #fff !default;
$stable:                        #f8f8f8 !default;
$positive:                      #4a87ee !default;
$calm:                          #43cee6 !default;
$balanced:                      #66cc33 !default;
$energized:                     #f0b840 !default;
$assertive:                     #ef4e3a !default;
$royal:                         #8a6de9 !default;
$dark:                          #444 !default;
```

Moreover, background classes have been defined with the latter color names prefixed. For example, a red background can be achieved by applying the `assertive-bg` class.

Later in this chapter you will learn how to use Sass to override Ionic Sass variables, such as the values of different colors delimited by `!default`. Overriding variables is an effective way of changing the look of built-in components without needing to write additional styling code.

Content spacing has been simplifed with the inclusion of CSS classes in the form of rows, columns, and padding. These classes provide consistent spacing sizes that are applied throughout Ionic and its various components. The `row` and `col`-prefixed classes allow for an easy grid-like organization of your application's content. They are built on the new CSS3 flexbox standard, and function as "flexible boxes" that take the maximum amount of space possible without skewing its inner content. Moreover, these classes are easily extensible since they rely heavily on variables to maintain consistency. For instance, the inherited value of `padding`-prefixed classes is defined by the `$content-padding` variable, which by default carries the value of `10px`. It suffices to modify the `$content-padding` variable to affect the entire layout of your Ionic application. Similarly, doubling the default `$item-padding` will have visual repercussions throughout the platform.

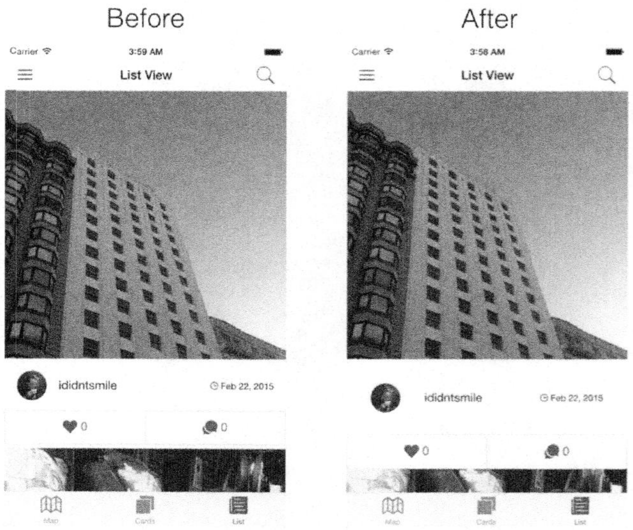

Further information and use cases about the Sass customization of design components used in the Trendicity application will be provided in the *Using Sass in Trendicity* section of this chapter.

Designing Trendicity

In developing Trendicity, we decided to restrain ourselves to mostly using core Ionic components in order to show the enormous breadth of design opportunities that comes packaged within the SDK. Fundamentally, this goes to show that Ionic is suitable for creating compelling mobile user interfaces without having to specify your own styling.

The utility classes mentioned in the previous section can be found scattered throughout our application. One particular use case of built-in color classes can be found in the **tab-list** view where we apply the **button-assertive** class in order to highlight the "Like" button in red whenever a user likes a post:

```
<div class="button-bar bar-light">
    <button class="button"
            ng-click="like($index)"
            ng-style="{ 'button-assertive':
post.user_has_liked }">
            <i class="icon ion-heart"></i>
            {{ post.likes.count | number }}
    </button>
    <button class="button">
        <i class="icon ion-chatbubbles"></i>
        {{ post.comments.count | number }}
    </button>
</div>
```

Another interesting thing to note is the use of the `has-header` class on most `ion-content` tags. This class pushes the view's content down by a default of 44px and serves as a way to ensure the visibility of the application's header bar. In most cases, you could define a header bar yourself and not have to apply the **has-header** class on the content that follows, similar to what we did in the login modal view. However, since the majority of our views are either children views of a side menu or tabular navigation structure, we push the **ion-view**'s content down by the size of the detached navigation bar defined in either **home** or **menu** views. Note that as of the latest releases, Ionic takes care of this automatically for you.

Ionic supports many developer-friendly shortcuts when using core components. These alternative ways of implementing certain features in your application can shorten the amount of markup required to create, say, a button with an icon. One straightforward way of creating such a button would be to define the button tag and the icon tag separately and including the latter in the former, like this:

```
<button class="button">
    <i class="icon ion-navicon"></i>
</button>
```

A shorthand way of defining these types of buttons can be achieved by applying the **button-icon** class and including icon-specific classes within the same button. An example of this implementation is located in the home view's navigation buttons, where we defined the menu button like so:

```
<button menu-toggle="left"
        class="button button-icon icon ion-navicon"></button>
```

Note the use of both **button-icon** and **icon** classes within the button are required to achieve this effect.

Ionicons

Ionic comes packaged with a custom font that serves as an iconset for your applications. In essence, Ionicons is a font built by the Ionic team for use as icons. Similar to other common alternatives on the web, such as Font Awesome, Ionicons enhance the visual appeal of your apps and are meant to be used to guide the user through the various actionable elements contained in your applications. The benefit of Ionicons is its ability to scale in size while maintaining the same high-fidelity image. Since it is fundamentally a font type, you can manipulate it using stylesheets like any other font, meaning you can increase the icon's size with the `font-size` property in CSS. Furthermore, additional Ionicons are regularly provided with new Ionic releases.

The iconset consists of four main collections: generic (platform independent) icons, iOS and Android inspired icons, as well as a handful of social media icons. Ionic also provides a CSS class aptly named `icon`, which allows you to incorporate the full-breadth of Ionicons in your application's UI components. For instance, to display the login icon in our application's side menu, use the HTML icon tag in the following manner: `<i class="icon ion-log-in"></i>`.

Ionicons also feature CSS3-animated icons, which are excellent for use as loading indicators. We used the new `ion-spinner`'s default icon in the `$ionicLoading` template as can be seen in `www/js/app.js`:

```
.constant('$ionicLoadingConfig', {
  template: '<ion-spinner></ion-spinner>
            Loading...'
})
```

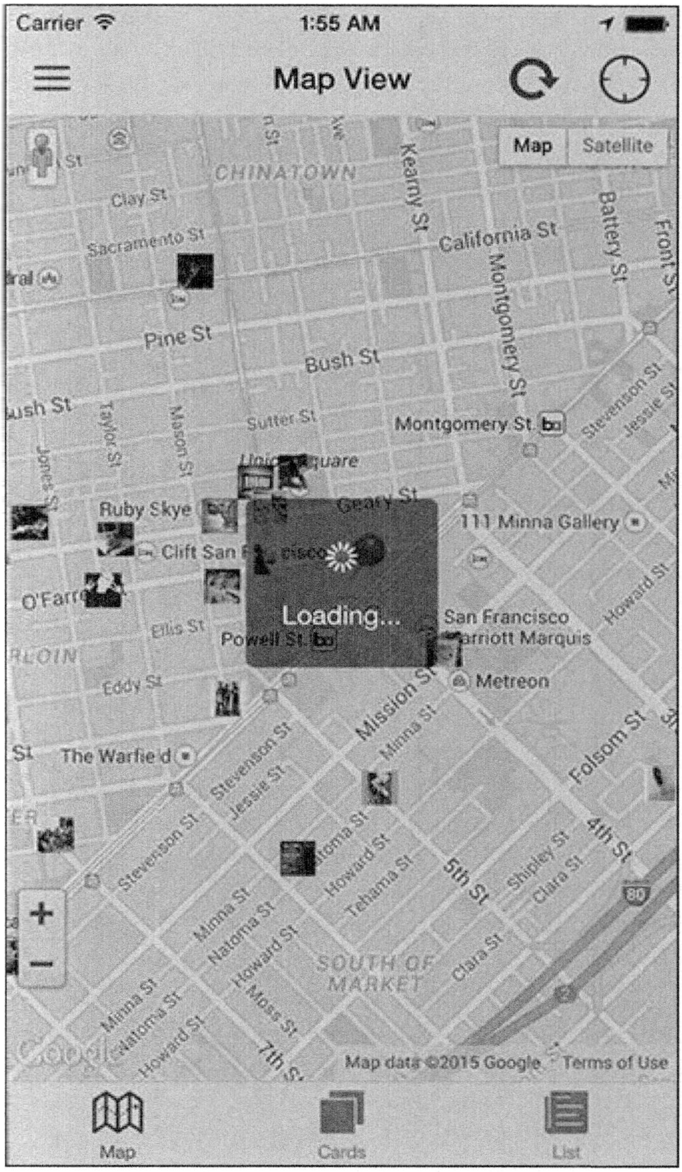

Due to Ionicons' nature as a font, you must place the provided Ionic fonts in the `www/fonts` directory to assure the proper functionality of your Ionic app. In Trendicity, our iconset has been modified to accomodate for the newest version of Ionicons 2.0. In this latest release, additional icons have been created, but most importantly iOS icons have been renamed from `ios7-` to `ios`-prefixed classes. In order to access all the new icon classes, we imported the entire Ionicons library by doing: `@import "www/lib/ionicons/scss/ionicons";`. Given that Ionicons are located inside of the `www` folder, we can simply point to the fonts located at `www/lib/ionicons/fonts`. However, this path must be relative to your CSS files. In our case, given that our CSS files are found in the `www/css` directory, the appropriate font path would be `../lib/ionicons/fonts`. Note that by default, when creating an Ionic project from the three main templates (`blank`, `sidemenu`, and `tabs`), the correct font path should already be defined. Similarly, when setting up a new project using Sass by doing `$ ionic setup sass`, the font path will be accurate as well.

With the latest release of Ionic's version 1 release candidate, the addition of the `ion-spinner` directive allows for SVG-based rotating spinners to be displayed, bypassing the Ionicons font altogether. Actually, since the second version of Ionicons was introduced, the spinning icons have been deprecated. Therefore, using `ion-spinner` is now the way to go when including loading icons in your Ionic apps.

Creating native-looking applications

To make your application stand out, we recommend using a combination of the provided `ionic.Platform` and its `isIOS()` and `isAndroid()` functions to determine the mobile device's operating system, and display the corresponding icons to really achieve the native application look. Moreover, you could incorporate a custom directive to automatically select the appropriate icon depending on the platform. In our application, we have provided you with an Angular directive created by Anton Shevchenko, one of our authors, located in `lib/ionic-contrib-icon/ionic.icon.js`, which allows you to specify different icons depending on the platform. For example, one use case can be found in our application's side menu: `<icon ios="ion-ios-home" default="ion-home"></icon>`. In essence, this directive checks the current device's platform using `ionic.Platform` and then applies the corresponding icon provided by the `ios`, `android` and `default` attributes. Note that you should always include a default icon, which will be applied during development in browsers or if no particular icon has been defined for the current device's platform.

As a side note, Ionic appends a platform specific class on the body of your application's `index.html` after having built it for a particular platform. Diving deeper into the `010_add_platform.js` Cordova hook, note that the script is triggered on the `after_prepare` event which occurs when running the following command: `$ ionic build [platform]`, where `[platform]` can be `ios`, `android`, or any other platform supported by Ionic. Interestingly, it is precisely the addition of these platform specific classes such as `.platform-ios` and `.platform-android` that are used to simulate different platforms in the browser when using Ionic Lab.

Customizing Ionic with Sass

Ionic is built with extensibility in mind. From the ground up, Ionic uses Sass as its preferred preprocessor for CSS styling, enabling developers like you more flexbility in terms of overriding the provided default styles. All variables used by the Ionic SDK have been conveniently defined and assembled in one file located at `www/lib/ionic/scss/_variables.scss`. Moreover, the variables are organized by the components that they target such as: buttons, bars, lists, forms, input fields, and more. In turn, doing things like changing the default height of all buttons in your application can be painlessly achieved by redefining the `$button-height` variable.

In this section, we will explore how you can employ Sass to easily adapt Ionic's component styling to your application's needs.

Overriding Ionic design with Sass

Knowing that Ionic's styles are all written in Sass, the predefined classes of the SDK can be effortlessly integrated in your project by importing them using `@import "www/lib/ionic/scss/ionic";`. Looking at Ionic's Sass variable definitions located at `www/lib/ionic/scss/_variables.scss`, we can notice the appended `!default` rule included with each variable. This allows you to specify a value of your choosing which will be applied instead of the default values specified in Ionic.

The proper way of going about overriding these variables is to specify their values before importing Ionic into your project. For instance, you could add the following to your main Sass file to enlarge the default text font size and lighten the character weight of headings:

```
// Define variable values
$font-size-base: 16px;
$headings-font-weight: 300;

// Import Ionic's styles
@import "www/lib/ionic/scss/ionic";
```

These values will replace the corresponding `!default` values defined in Ionic's `_variables.scss` file.

Furthermore, Ionic provides scores of Sass mixins that work like containers of reusable CSS styles and can be included with the **`@include`** keyword in your own Sass files. These blocks of code can act as "helper functions" as they can be passed parameters to generate the styling you want. Once again, Ionic has defined all of its mixins in one conveniently named file located at `www/lib/ionic/scss/_mixins.scss`.

Looking at some of Ionic's source code, we can see integral mixins being used by core components such as buttons, bars, list items, tabs, and animations.

In order to become more familiar with how Ionic's mixins can be used, let us examine how the `button-light` class works by applying various mixins. Knowing how to properly use mixins will prove very important in our implementation of the `vertical-center` class defined in the next section of this chapter.

Let us begin our analysis of Ionic's use of Sass mixins by extracting the pieces of styling attributed to the `button-light` class:

```
.button {
    // set the color defaults
    @include button-style($button-default-bg,
                          $button-default-border,
                          $button-default-active-bg,
                          $button-default-active-border,
                          $button-default-text);

    ...

    &.button-light {
        @include button-style($button-light-bg,
                              $button-light-border,
                              $button-light-active-bg,
                              $button-light-active-border,
                              $button-light-text);
        @include button-clear($button-light-border);
        @include button-outline($button-light-border);
    }
```

```
    ...
}
```

We notice that `button-light` is nested in the `button` class with an appended &. Therefore, this class will only be applied on a component whenever the `button` class is also present. For instance the following will not work:

```
<button class="button-light">.button-light</button>
```

On the other hand, applying the `button button-light` classes will generate our desired effect properly:

```
<button class="button button-light">.button.button-light</
button>
```

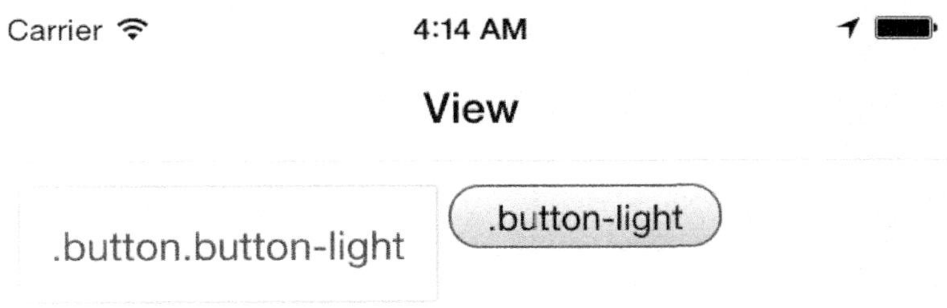

The default `button` class is important as it includes the `button-style` mixin which will define the general look of an Ionic button by passing the `$button-default-bg, ..., $button-default-text` arguments into the `button-style` mixin:

```
@mixin button-style($bg-color,
                    $border-color,
                    $active-bg-color,
                    $active-border-color,
                    $color) {
    border-color: $border-color;
    background-color: $bg-color;
    color: $color;

    // Give desktop users something to play with
    &:hover {
```

```
            color: $color;
            text-decoration: none;
        }
        &.active,
        &.activated {
            border-color: $active-border-color;
            background-color: $active-bg-color;
            box-shadow: inset 0px 1px 3px rgba(0,0,0,0.15);
        }
    }
```

Consequently, after having compiled the code with Sass, the final output of the button class will look like this:

```
    .button {
        border-color: #b2b2b2;
        background-color: #f8f8f8;
        color: #444;

        // Give desktop users something to play with
        &:hover {
            color: #444;
            text-decoration: none;
        }
        &.active,
        &.activated {
            border-color: #a2a2a2;
            background-color: #e5e5e5;
            box-shadow: inset 0px 1px 3px rgba(0,0,0,0.15);
        }

        ...
    }
```

Note that, by default, Ionic uses the `button-default` colors for the `button` class. Knowing that all variables, including the colors, are defined in the `_variables.scss` file, it becomes a breeze to change the colors of the default button by simpy overriding the `$button-default`-prefixed variables to colors of your choosing, without affecting other button color classes.

The walkthrough we just did was only for the `button` class, not the `button-light` class. However, with our accumulated knowledge of mixins, we may conclude that the same concept applies to the `button-light` class, with `$button-light`-prefixed variables being sent as arguments to the `button-style` mixin.

Additionally, button-clear and button-outline mixins are included to define the light button's look when applied with the button-clear and button-outline classes.

With our enhanced knowledge of mixins, and with further accommodation to Ionic's Sass structure and variables, you will become accustomed to integrating these handy shortcuts at your choosing to cut down on the amount of code required to style components.

Lastly, compiling your Sass code can be achieved by setting up your project using the following Ionic CLI commands:

```
$ ionic setup sass
$ gulp sass
```

By default, setting up Sass in this way will cause your .scss files located at scss/ to be watched automatically and recompiled when running your application using $ ionic serve. In essence, the gulp sass task is automatically run and the scss/ directory is watched whenever developing locally. These tasks and watch patterns are defined in the ionic.project file. Feel free to add or modify the existing tasks to be executed when serving your app to the browser.

Using Sass in Trendicity

Integrating Sass into our application was fairly easy to do. In order to define and compile Sass styles, we simply used Ionic's built-in setup by running $ ionic setup sass in the terminal. This command creates a top-level directory named scss/ and by default includes an ionic.app.scss file that imports the Ionic Sass library and configures the font path automatically. We created new Sass files as we needed them by prefixing the filenames with an underscore and importing them in the main ionic.app.scss file.

In terms of structuring, we settled on a similar approach to Ionic's Sass styles structure, through organizing our files by the components they target as well as grouping all variables in _variables.scss file.

Including Sass in our project gave us access to all of Ionic's mixins and variables. This way our styling could be consistent with predefined values of the SDK. For instance, we used the $light variable as the popup's background color. Our overridden slider-slide class applied the $font-family-light-sans-serif font.

Moreover, our design goal for the login modal was to center the content in the middle of the view. To go about this, we could have created a custom directive to calculate the total height of the screen and adjust the positioning of our content accordingly. However, we decided to go with a cleaner CSS-only approach leveraging the new `flexbox` standard:

```
.vertical-center-container {
    height: 100%;

    display: -webkit-box;
    display: -moz-box;
    display: -ms-flexbox;
    display: -webkit-flex;
    display: flex;
    -webkit-justify-content: center;
    -ms-flex-pack: center;
    justify-content: center;
    -webkit-box-align: center;
    -moz-box-align: center;
    -webkit-align-items: center;
    -ms-flex-align: center;
    align-items: center;

    .vertical-center {
        width: 100%;

        display: -webkit-box;
        display: -moz-box;
        display: -ms-flexbox;
        display: -webkit-flex;
        display: flex;
        -webkit-flex-direction: column;
        -ms-flex-direction: column;
        flex-direction: column;
    }
}
```

Looking at this block of code, we tried to simplify it. This is where examining the various mixins available in the Ionic SDK as part of the previous section really pays off.

Finally, we applied the necessary Sass mixins and reduced our initial styling to something a lot more reasonable:

```
.vertical-center-container {
    height: 100%;
```

```
        @include display-flex();
        @include justify-content(center);
        @include align-items(center);

        .vertical-center {
            width: 100%;

            @include display-flex();
            @include flex-direction(column);
        }
    }
```

f we hadn't peeked at Ionic's source code, we would have either stayed with the initial block of code, or would have resorted to defining our own Sass mixins.

Also, note the similarity between our approach towards vertical centering and how the Ionic popup and loading components are centered on the screen. Taking a peek at the source code, we find that both the popup-container and loading-container classes include the same three mixins we used in our vertical-center-container class:

```
.popup-container {
    ...

    @include display-flex();
    @include justify-content(center);
    @include align-items(center);

    ...
}

...

.loading-container {
    ...

    @include display-flex();
    @include justify-content(center);
    @include align-items(center);

    ...
}
```

To wrap up, the integration of Sass in Trendicity allowed our styling code to become more coherent as we took advantage of Sass' selector nesting, used the provided Ionic mixins and variables, and defined our very own reusuable variables, such as $login-margin and $list-margin.

Gotchas

It may occur to you that in some instances Ionic's default styling does not align with your intentions. For instance, knowing that the $light color is assigned the color white by default, you would assume that a clear light button would be white when defined like so:

```
<button class="button button-clear button-light">
    ...
</button>
```

However, looking at Ionic's Sass source code, you will see that the combination of button-clear and button-light classes will apply a color defined by the $button-light-border variable.

For our login modal, we wanted to have a clear white button on the top-right corner. To achieve this, we added the following Sass styling in our _button.scss file:

```
.button {
    &.button-light {
        &.button-clear {
            color: $light;
        }
    }
}
```

Here is a before and after comparison:

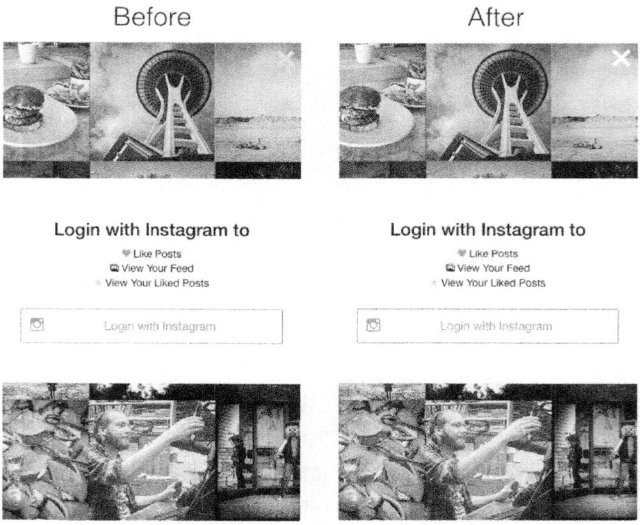

Instead of writing our own class for this particular situation, we could have simply overriden the $button-light-border variable to contain the value of the white color. No other changes would have been required. However, note that overriding any Ionic variable may impact other components because these variables are used throughout the SDK's Sass styles. In this scenario, changing the $button-light-border color to $light would have caused the side menu's item borders to blend with the white background of the menu view. This is why we opted to solely override the combination of `button-clear` and `button-light` classes.

Many new directives have been integrated into the Ionic SDK such as `ion-content`, `ion-list`, `ion-item`, and `ion-checkbox` to only name the common ones. It is always important to consider them as predefined building blocks, which are meant to improve workflow and efficiency. Flexibility is inherently limited with these directives because of their nature of following a predefined structure. These components are built on top of the robust collection of CSS classes such as `content`, `list`, `item`, `item-checkbox`, and `checkbox`, which can always be assembled in various ways by yourself to achieve the look and feel you require.

Another frequently-mentioned problem pertains to particular scenarios that have caused weird issues with Ionic's JavaScript-based scrolling system. In essence, in particular situations, the scroller might not display the complete view contained in the `ion-content` section of your template, cutting off the bottom of the container (usually) by a few pixels. In fact, it has been determined that it was precisely the amount of pixels defined by the margins applied with components such as buttons and paragraphs. Based on the amount of activity on Ionic's forums, this issue has been faced by a significant amount of developers and is deemed relevant to reveal in this chapter. One fix that has been proven to work is to apply padding to the containing `ion-content` directive, or to wrap all your components in a `div` with the `padding` class.

An additional issue affecting the scrolling system is the use of `ng-hide` and `ng-show` attributes, again in particular cases only. For instance, hiding or displaying components when your content overflows the screen may not cause the scrollable view to refresh its vertical position. This is where the provided `$ionicScrollDelegate`'s `resize()` function comes in handy. This function recalculates your content's actual size in the view, and adjusts the scroll position accordingly.

Bugs aside, the team behind Ionic and the broader open source developer community are constantly fleshing out these issues.

Extending Ionic

Ionic's greatness is not only defined by its ease of use, plug'n play components and other provided help in the form of forums and documentation. The community is what really makes it stand out compared to other hybrid mobile development SDK's and frameworks. In terms of components, the community has seen the advent of skillful component implementations, which purposefully enhance the functionality of Ionic applications. In fact, numerous developers have contributed by providing great design additions that build upon Ionic's solid base. In essence, these contributions are *extensions* of the core SDK.

Noteworthy additions include `ionic-contrib-swipe-cards`, `ionic-contrib-ios-rounded-buttons`, `ionic-contrib-header-shrink`, `ionic-contrib-frost` and a new iteration of swipe cards called `ionic-contrib-tinder-cards` just to name a few. Interestingly, during the development of Trendicity, our very own Keith Moore enhanced the `tinder-cards` functionality, which ended up being used in our application's card view.

Lastly, we recommend harnessing AngularJS's power to your advantage in order to build upon Ionic's core functionality. Be sure to create custom directives and services to unleash the full capacity of the Ionic development platform.

Summary

In this chapter, we focused on Ionic's design components, exploring the vast array of provided styles, tools and building blocks available to hybrid mobile app developers. Because Ionic's official documentation as yet does not include every one of the interesting components we unearthed, there is immense benefit to examining the source code. For example, background color classes and numerous mixins will probably be useful in the future. We also touched upon the Sass preprocessor technology, which greatly enhances workflow and can reduce code complexity with the use of mixins and variables. Finally, we delved into the integration of Sass with Ionic in the development of the Trendicity application.

In the next chapter, we will familiarize ourselves on the Instagram API and find out how Trendicity works in order to fetch posts based on location and popularity, as well as handling user actions such as liking images.

Implementing a side menu and setting up the routes 5

A sliding side menu has become one of the most well known UI elements in mobile applications. In its most typical implementation, a side menu consists of a *menu view* in the background, and the *content view* on top of that *menu view*. A user can either swipe the content away to display the side menu, or click (or tap) a toggle button to do so. To build a side menu using Ionic, we will be using a set of predefined directives, which will handle most of the logic we just described.

The most important directives we will be using are:

- `<ion-side-menus>`
- `<ion-side-menu-content>`
- `<ion-side-menu>`

These directives will be handling all of the magic that comes with side menu logic in our Trendicity application. Positioned on either the left or right side of the screen, or both, a side menu handles an important part of your application's navigation.

Introduction to Ionic's side menu directives

First, let's go ahead and take a look at the side menu view as we built it for Trendicity. From there on we will go through the code by breaking down every step of the process.

For starters we take a look at the end result. The side menu in Trendicity looks like this in a browser:

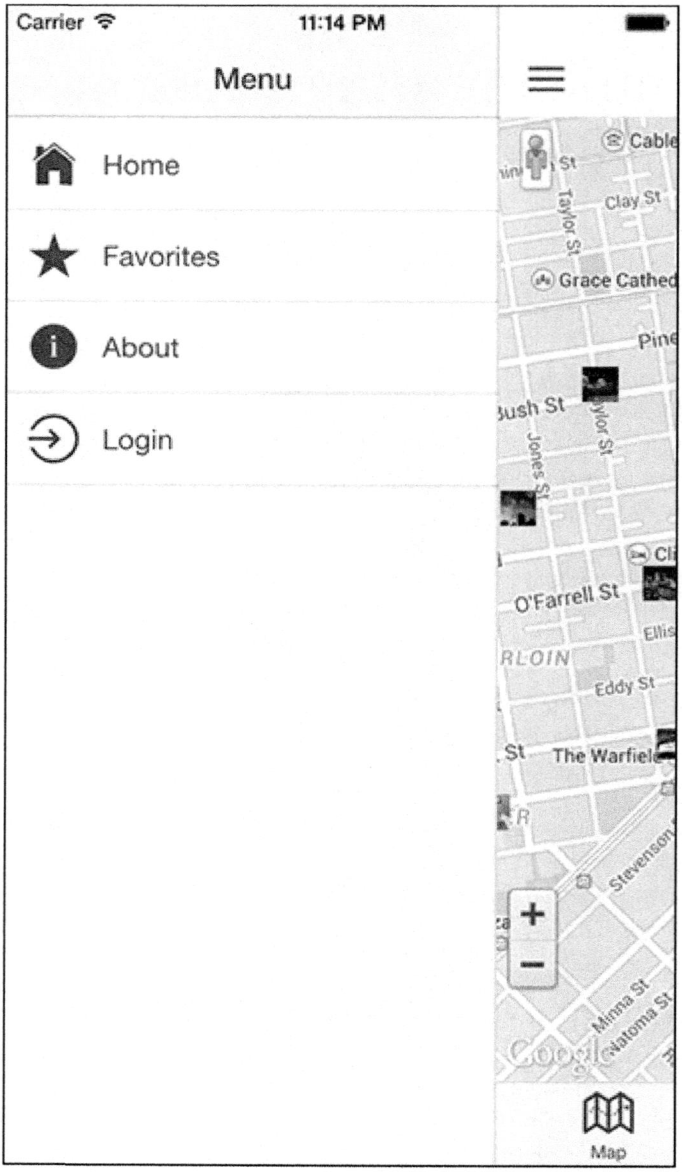

We have all of the common UI elements right in place: a header bar with the menu title, a menu toggle, which moved to the right when the menu opened, and the menu content contains a list of menu items.

To achieve this result, the following Ionic template was used:

```
// /www/templates/menu.html
<ion-side-menus enable-menu-with-back-views="false">

  <ion-side-menu-content>
    <ion-nav-bar class="bar-stable">
        <ion-nav-buttons side="left">
            <button class="button button-icon button-clear
ion-navicon" menu-toggle="left"></button>
        </ion-nav-buttons>
    </ion-nav-bar>
    <ion-nav-view name="menuContent" animation="slide-left-
right"></ion-nav-view>
  </ion-side-menu-content>

  <ion-side-menu side="left">
    <ion-header-bar class="bar-stable">
          <h1 class="title">Menu</h1>
    </ion-header-bar>
    <ion-content class="has-header">
      <ion-list>
        <ion-item menu-close class="item-icon-left" ui-
sref="app.home.map" ui-sref-opts="{ reload: true,
inherit:false }">
          <icon ios="ion-ios-home" default="ion-home"></icon>
          Home
        </ion-item>
        <ion-item menu-close class="item-icon-left" ui-
sref="app.favorites">
          <icon ios="ion-ios-star" default="ion-star"></icon>
          Favorites
        </ion-item>
        <ion-item menu-close class="item-icon-left" ui-
sref="app.intro">
          <icon ios="ion-ios-information" default="ion-
information-circled"></icon>
          About
        </ion-item>
        <ion-item menu-close class="item-icon-left" ng-
click="login()" ng-hide="isLoggedIn()">
            <i class="icon ion-log-in"></i>
            Login
        </ion-item>
        <ion-item menu-close class="item-icon-left" ng-
click="logout()" ng-show="isLoggedIn()">
            <i class="icon ion-log-out"></i>
            Logout
        </ion-item>
      </ion-list>
    </ion-content>
```

```
    </ion-side-menu>
  </ion-side-menus>
```

ion-side-menus

The first directive we will come across is the `ion-side-menus` directive. It is a container element for side menus and the main content. It also allows the left and/or right side menu to be toggled by dragging the main content area from either left to right, to open the left menu, or right to left to open the right menu if that menu is defined. In Trendicity we set the optional attribute `enable-menu-with-back-views` to `false` in order to disable the side menu toggle when we're inside a nested view that has a back button.

ion-side-menu-content

A part of the side menu structure we have defined is the `ion-side-menu-content` directive. This is a container for the main visible content, sibling to one or more `ionSideMenu` directives. This directive can either be used as a standalone element or as an attribute of another directive or element. In the example, `ion-side-menu-content` is setup as an attribute of a `ion-pane` element.

```
<ion-side-menu>
<!-- ion-pane contents -->
</ion-side-menu>
```

`ion-pane` is a simple directive that contains content, with no side effects.

DISABLING CONTENT DRAGGING TO OPEN THE SIDE MENU

By default, a user can drag the content of the app from left to right to open the side menu. To disable such behavior, the `ion-side-menu-content` directive offers an optional attribute called `drag-content`, which can be set to `false` to disable this behavior. For Trendicity, we have not defined a custom setting for this attribute and rely on its default `true` value.

For further customization of this behavior, such as whether the content drag can only start if it is below a certain threshold distance from the edge of the screen, check out **the documentation**.

ion-side-menu

Next up is the big guy, `ion-side-menu` itself. The `ion-side-menu` directive should always be a child of the `ion-side-menus` directive. By using this directive you can define either a left or right side menu. To specify the position of the side menu, use the `side` attribute like so:

```
<ion-side-menu side="left">
<!-- side menu content like a header and a list of menu
items -->
</ion-side-menu>
```

The `side` attribute takes either 'left' or 'right' as an allowed value. The side menu's width is set by default to 275 pixels. If you want to customize this width, simply use the `width` attribute to do so.

```
<ion-side-menu side="left" width="200 + extraPadding">
<!-- side menu content like a header and a list of menu
items -->
</ion-side-menu>
```

As shown above, width accepts any **valid AngularJS expression**. For more details about valid expressions, check out **Expressions** in the AngularJS documentation: **https://docs.angularjs.org/guide/expression**.

PROGRAMMATICALLY DISABLING THE SIDE MENU

There might be some cases where you want to disable the side menu, such as when your side menu contains content which is only enabled for logged in users. Or perhaps your user should finish a certain case first before you want to enable the side menu. In these specific cases, Ionic provides an extra attribute called `is-enabled`. As with most Ionic attributes, it takes a valid AngularJS expression as its value. For instance, a scope method that validates the `isLoggedIn` state:

```
<ion-side-menu side="left" width="200 + extraPadding" is-
enabled="isLoggedIn()">
<!-- side menu content like a header and a list of menu
items -->
</ion-side-menu>
```

In the example above, we call the `isLoggedIn()` method in order to check if the side menu should be enabled or not.

For Trendicity, we have not defined a custom side menu width or a specific case where the side menu should be disabled, as you can see in our template file above.

Within the `<ion-side-menu>` directive, we can design our side menu just the way we want. You can think of the `<ion-side-menu>` content as just another view in your application. That is exactly how the main menu in Trendicity is built: a basic view with a header, content, and list directive to show the menu items.

ion-header-bar

First up is the `<ion-header-bar>` directive. It resembles the header element in our application and has some neat mobile-friendly features built right in there like *tap-to-scroll*, and proper title alignment so that you won't have to figure that out yourself.

The *tap-to-scroll* feature is very straight forward. When a user touches the header bar, the `<ion-content>` element will scroll back to the top, the same way that many other apps handle that behavior. Of course like with most default behavior, there is a way to turn this off. That can be done by adding the `no-tap-scroll` attribute to the `<ion-header-bar>` directive and setting its value to `true` like so:

```
<ion-header-bar align-title="left" no-tap-scroll="true"
class="bar-stable">
    <h1 class="title">Menu</h1>
</ion-header-bar>
```

Since we actually want *tap-to-scroll* in our side menu, you will not be finding this particular attribute in the sample code because its value is set to `false` by default, which enables tap to scroll.

ALIGNING THE HEADER TITLE

Using the `align-title` attribute on `<ion-header-bar>` you are able to align the header's title properly. By default this alignment happens platform dependent. That means that on iOS, the header's title will align to the center and on the Android platform the text will align to the left. The `align-title` attribute takes either `'left'`, `'right'`, or `'center'` as valid values for the corresponding alignment.

Wrapping up the side menu

We have now set up all the required directives to handle side menu logic in our application. We started off by the top-level `<ion-side-menus>` directive, which contains `<ion-side-menu>` directives and the `<ion-pane>` directive that holds the main application content.

LAST BUT NOT LEAST

There is one small but important part of the example code we have not paid attention to yet. That is the `menu-close` directive. It is an attribute only directive, which can be added to clickable elements. In Trendicity we have given each menu item the `menu-close` directive, which causes, as one might expect, the side menu to close as soon as one of these links is tapped.

In some situations we might not want the menu to close when something inside the `<ion-side-menu>` directive is tapped. For instance, we might want to open up a sub menu or start sorting list items. That is why the `menu-close` directive was introduced to force this behavior manually.

As you might have noticed when we set up the menu items with the `<ion-item>` directives, there was an unknown attribute directive used called `ui-sref`. It seems familiar to an anchor element's `href` attribute and does indeed point to a specific part of the application. These definitions are called routes, which we will set up in the next chapter using Angular UI's UI-Router component.

Handling routes with the Angular UI Router component

Ionic uses the Angular UI Router module so application interfaces can be organized into various *states*. Since handling routes and defining states in particular is not an actual part of Ionic, this chapter will shortly cover the basics of setting up routes with Angular UI's **Router component**. At the moment of writing, the Angular UI Router component is one of the most popular methods to set up advanced routing logic for your AngularJS application.

About Angular UI

Angular UI is an organization that originally started off as one project to consolidate efforts people were making early on across the entire community to create defacto widgets and directives for AngularJS (like jQueryUI is to jQuery). Although it started off as one project with multiple widget wrappers, it's evolved into an organization with multiple teams and projects with different focuses.

The future of AngularJS application routing

Please note that this book was written and the companion app Trendicity was built when AngularJS 1.3 was just recently released. For the future AngularJS 2.0, a new router is being developed that is also backported to AngularJS 1.3. Similar to Angular UI Router, the new router is also based on (nestable) states. However, it is up to Drifty to incorporate support for that router in Ionic.

Setting up the application routes

Aside from some one-time setup logic, the `app.js` file (which can be found in `www/js/app.js`) contains all of the application's routing logic as well. This logic is defined using the aforementioned `UI Router` component and its `$stateProvider` and `$urlRouterProvider` providers.

First, let us take a look at the complete routing setup as it is used in Trendicity.

```
// ... app.js configuration code above

.config(function($stateProvider, $urlRouterProvider) {
  $stateProvider
    .state('app', {
      url: '/app',
      abstract: true,
      templateUrl: 'templates/menu.html',
      controller: 'AppCtrl'
    })

    .state('app.intro', {
      url: '/intro',
      views: {
        'menuContent': {
          templateUrl: 'templates/intro.html',
```

```
      controller: 'IntroCtrl'
    }
  }
})

.state('app.favorites', {
  url: '/favorites',
  views: {
    'menuContent': {
      templateUrl: 'templates/favorites.html',
      controller: 'FavoritesCtrl'
    }
  }
})

.state('app.home', {
  url: '/home',
  abstract: true,
  views: {
    'menuContent': {
      templateUrl: 'templates/home.html',
      controller: 'HomeCtrl'
    }
  }
})

.state('app.home.map', {
  url: '/map/?latitude&longitude',
  views: {
    'tab-map': {
      templateUrl: 'templates/tab-map.html',
      controller: 'MapViewCtrl as mapCtrl'
    }
  }
})

.state('app.home.card', {
  url: '/card',
  views: {
    'tab-card': {
      templateUrl: 'templates/tab-card.html',
      controller: 'CardViewCtrl'
    }
  }
})

.state('app.home.list', {
  url: '/list',
  views: {
```

```
          'tab-list': {
            templateUrl: 'templates/tab-list.html',
            controller: 'ListViewCtrl'
          }
        }
      });

  // if none of the above states are matched, use this as
the fallback
  $urlRouterProvider.otherwise('/app/home/map/');
})

// ... app.js continues here
```

Defining the root state

In the routing setup we see a couple of different configurations. The first one is fairly simple.

```
.state('app', {
  url: '/app',
  abstract: true,
  templateUrl: 'templates/menu.html',
  controller: 'AppCtrl'
})
```

Here we define the state name and a URL is defined with the value /app. One thing you might have noticed is the `abstract` key in the configuration object. Setting `abstract` to `true` means, as one might expect, that this defined state is actually an abstract state. An abstract state can have child states but can not get activated itself. An `abstract` state is simply a state that can't be transitioned to. It is activated implicitly when one of its descendants are activated. This means that we cannot specifically open the /app route in our application.

For more details about abstract states and how to use them, read the **excellent documentation** from the Angular UI team and contributors.

Defining a state with named view and custom template and controller

Next we have defined a named state like this one:

```
.state('app.home', {
    url: '/home',
```

```
        abstract: true,
        views: {
            'menuContent' :{
                templateUrl: 'templates/home.html',
                controller: 'HomeCtrl'
            }
        }
    })
```

One thing you might notice is that we have defined the `views` property in the state's configuration object this time. Using the `views` property allows us to define custom template files and optional controllers for *named views*.

You might still remember this part from the previous chapter when we have built the side menu template file:

```
<ion-side-menu-content>
    <ion-nav-bar class="bar-stable">
        <ion-nav-buttons side="left">
            <button
                class="button button-icon button-clear ion-
navicon"
                menu-toggle="left">
            </button>
        </ion-nav-buttons>
    </ion-nav-bar>
    <ion-nav-view
        name="menuContent"
        animation="slide-left-right">
    </ion-nav-view>
</ion-side-menu-content>
```

In there, we have defined the `<ion-nav-view>` directive with the name `menuContent`. As mentioned, Ionic plays very nice with Angular UI s Router component. The name of the view we have defined here is the exact same name of the view we mentioned in the previous code example where we have set up a named view.

Let's break down the code example step-by-step. First we define the state and it's custom route like we have done before. Then we add the *views* property to the configuration object:

```
.state('app.home', {
    url: '/home',
    abstract: true,
    views: {
```

```
            'menuContent': {
                templateUrl: 'templates/home.html',
                controller: 'HomeCtrl'
            }
        }
    })
```

By using the name of the view we have defined previously as a key in our configuration object, we tell the router that we want to load the template `templates/home.html` in the `menuContent` view and manage it using the controller `HomeCtrl`.

Finished routing Trendicity

By now you should be familiar with setting up routes for your next Ionic project using the UI-Router component from the Angular UI team. You know how you could inherit the scope to different sub views by setting up nested routes. Optionally you can provide an abstract route as a root for one of these nested routes.

Routing is something that you should think through before you get started with it. It is basically what connects all of the separate parts in your application together by defining how they are connected and how it would be possible for an end user to navigate to one of the many (nested) routes in your application.

Integrating a map view with Ionic 6

When we implemented Favorites in the previous chapter, the user was asked to provide a city and optional state or country where the favorite location should be. Then, by using the `GeolocationService` we've built for Trendicity, that input was converted to an object with latitude and longitude properties, which were stored in the favorite object.

These location details were needed to center the map view on to that particular location and retrieve nearby Instagram posts, which are shown as markers on the map. This map view is what we will be focusing on in this chapter. We will guide you through the forest of AngularJS Google Maps directives, and get you up and running with some fancy marker and positioning actions.

Picking an AngularJS directive for Google Maps

Ionic does not have a map directive built into the framework, but thankfully we can use a community directive without any issues. In the case of our example application, Trendicity, we selected a suitable Angular-based library that met three of our needs:

1. Google Maps as tile service
2. Fast performance on mobile devices
3. No need for offline capabilities

To be completely honest, this was probably the hardest part for us when building Trendicity. There is a wide variety of Google Maps related directives out in the wild. Their functionality defers from very basic `new google.maps.Map()` calls to complete asynchronous Google Maps v3

API loading and map initialization with nested directives for markers and polygons.

We will be covering a selection of three Google Maps Angular projects, and how you can easily implement a third-party library in your existing Ionic project in this chapter. We will also be covering Ionic's 'magic switch' `data-tap-disabled` and how, when, and why to apply it.

The candidates

Let's take a look at the candidate libraries.

ANGULAR-GOOGLE-MAPS

When searching online for 'angular google maps' you might come across the `angular-google-maps` library as one of your first results. It is another project by the Angular UI team and it's very well documented. The project is very much alive and has a large community using it. But then again, the usage of this particular directive and its nested directives for markers and marker windows can be tough to understand.

UI-MAPS

Confusingly, the same Angular UI team also has the `ui-maps` project. When we're snooping around on the GitHub repositories page we quickly notice there is something wrong with this project. As of this moment, the project has quite some open pull requests and was last updated over a year ago. That didn't give us much confidence in using it. Based on some community reports and a lengthy topic in the issues section we discovered that the Angular UI team discontinued this project in favor of `angular-google-maps`.

LEAFLETJS

Leaflet is something entirely different. It existed before we even started thinking about building hybrid apps with Angular. Leaflet is a widely used open source JavaScript library used to build web mapping applications. It supports most mobile and desktop platforms, supporting HTML5, and CSS3. Alongside OpenLayers and the Google Maps API, it is one of the most popular JavaScript mapping libraries, and is now used by major web sites such as FourSquare, Pinterest, and Flickr.

AND THE WINNER IS

... `angular-google-maps`. Why not Leaflet? Keeping in mind that we wanted to demonstrate implementing a Google Maps powered map to interact with it, `angular-google-maps` was the best choice. When we switched out the Open Street Maps tile provider with Google Maps when using Leaflet, there was a huge performance drop on both mobile and desktop. Considering the performance and the fact that we have no need to display tiles from an offline data source, Leaflet is great at that, we decided to go with `angular-google-maps`.

Note that there are plenty other Angular projects that implement Google Maps. This is just a selection of the many libraries that you can find out there.

Creating the geolocation utility service

Before we get started using the `angular-google-maps` library, we first take a look at the `GeolocationService`, which we already mentioned in Chapter 4. In the `GeolocationService` we have implemented three straight forward geolocation related methods.

One of these methods is the `getDefaultPosition()` method. As every good method name already suggests, this is a way to get the default location object. We use the method to return the fallback position, when retrieving the user's actual position fails for any reason. There's no rocket science here.

Implementing ngCordova and the $cordovaGeolocation service

Next up is the `getCurrentPosition()` method. This method returns a promise that will retrieve the user's current position using the `$cordovaGeolocation` service.

```
// GeolocationService
// /www/js/services/geolocation.js

this.getCurrentPosition = function () {
    var defer = $q.defer();

    $ionicPlatform.ready(function () {
        var posOptions = {timeout: 10000,
```

```
enableHighAccuracy: false};

        $cordovaGeolocation
            .getCurrentPosition(posOptions)
            .then(
                function (position) {
                    $log.debug('Got geolocation');
                    defer.resolve(position);
                },
                function (locationError) {
                    $log.debug('Did not get geolocation');

                    defer.reject({
                        code: locationError.code,
                        message: locationError.message,
                        coords: fallbackPositionObject
                    });
                }
            );
    });

    return defer.promise;
};
```

To mimic the same behavior as the `$cordovaGeolocation` service, we create a deferred object to return its promise later on. After that we will call `$cordovaGeolocation.getCurrentPosition()` to retrieve the users current location by leveraging their GPS hardware using the installed Cordova plugin from the ngCordova project. Following the instructions from **ngCordova website** we have installed the `org.apache.cordova.geolocation` Cordova plugin as follows:

```
$ ionic plugin add org.apache.cordova.geolocation
```

And of course we have installed the `ngCordova` project using Bower:

```
$ bower install --save ngCordova
```

$ionicPlatform.ready()

After the plugin is installed, we are able to fully leverage the `$cordova-Geolocation` service. A keen reader would have noticed by now that the `getCurrentPosition()` method of the `GeolocationService` is basically the same as the one from `$cordovaGeolocation`. Why bother creating a method that does exactly the same thing? There is one important difference and it's wrapped around `$cordovaGeolocation`: `$ionicPlatform`.

As you can see, we have wrapped `$cordovaGeolocation` inside of an `$ionicPlatform.ready()` callback. By doing so the `$cordovaGeolocation` service will start looking up the user's location when the device is actually ready to do so. When the application is within a *webview* (Cordova), it will fire the callback once the device is ready. If the application is within a web browser, it will fire the callback after the `window.load` event.

Converting addresses to geolocation objects using the Google Maps Geocode API

Next up is the `addressToPosition()` method. We have already used this in Chapter 4, and by now you know it is useful when you want to convert a certain address as a string to a geolocation object. The functionality is pretty straight forward: address as a string goes in, and geolocation comes out as a promise.

```
// GeolocationService
// /www/js/services/geolocation.js
this.addressToPosition = function (strAddress) {
    var geocodingApiUrl = 'http://maps.googleapis.com/
maps/api/geocode/json?address=' + strAddress +
'&sensor=false';

    var convertResultToLatLng = function (result) {
        var location =
result.data.results[0].geometry.location;

        // Transforming the 'location.lat' and 'location.lng'
        // object to 'location.latitude' to be compatible
with
        // other location responses like in
getCurrentPosition
        return {
            latitude: location.lat,
            longitude: location.lng
        }
    };

    return $http.get(geocodingApiUrl)
```

```
            .then(
                convertResultToLatLng,
                function (reason) {
                    return $q.reject(reason);
                }
            );
    };
```

Using Angular's `$http` service, we literally *get* the geolocation object from the Google Maps Geocode API. After retrieving a successful dataset, the specific latitude and longitude values are filtered out of the results and returned as an object for later use.

Setting up the map view inside a tab

Once we have the `GeolocationService` up and running we are ready to move on to the big guy, implementing `angular-google-maps` in the tab's view. The resulting view is shown below, and we will guide you step-by-step through its creation. Here is the map view as seen from a browser:

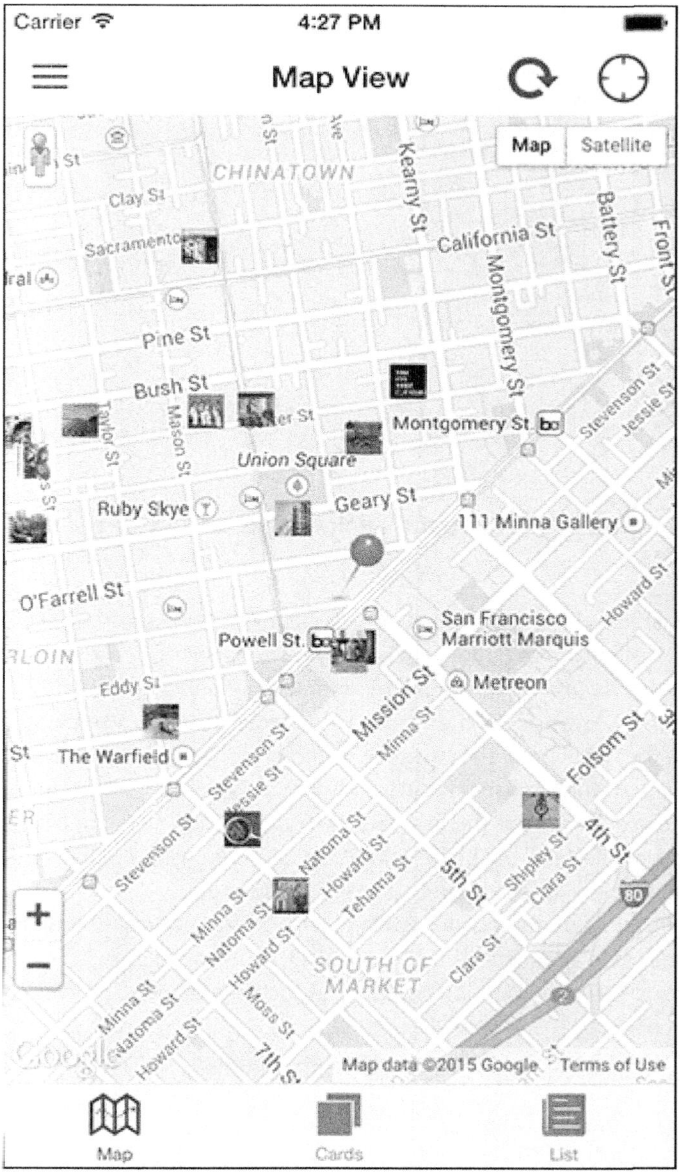

And, the HTML used to generate the map view:

```
// /www/templates/tap-map.html
<div data-tap-disabled="true" id="googleMap">
```

```
    <img class="map-pin-center" src="img/map-pin.png">
    <ui-gmap-google-map
        control="map.control"
        center="map.center"
        zoom="map.zoom">

        <ui-gmap-markers
            models="map.markers"
            coords="'coords'"
            icon="'icon'"
            click="'showPost'">
        </ui-gmap-markers>
    </ui-gmap-google-map>
</div>
```

We have omitted the wrapping `ion-content` directive in this example.

Touchstart, touchend, and click events on touch-enabled devices

Adam Bradley, one of the core developers of Ionic, wrote the following about the infamous 300ms click delay, also known as ‘ghost click’ or ‘fastclick’, which browsers implement for touch-enabled devices:

On touch devices such as a phone or tablet, browsers implement a 300ms delay between the time the user stops touching the display and the moment the browser executes the click. It was initially introduced so the browser can tell if the user wants to double-tap to zoom in on the web page. Basically, the browser waits roughly 300ms to see if the user is double-tapping, or just tapping on the display once.

Out of the box, Ionic automatically removes the 300ms delay in order to make Ionic applications feel more like native applictions. Other solutions, such as fastclick and Angular’s ngTouch should not be included, to avoid conflicts.

But Ionic is not the only one with a workaround for this behavior. As soon as you start developing a library that is mobile friendly, you will need to address this issue sooner or later when you start tweaking the performance.

Now we have two libraries handling the click events inside of our `<ion-content>` element. This can lead to unexpected or unwanted behavior like markers that can’t be clicked or that trigger an unwanted double click. Ionic has a built in workaround for situations like these, where you can’t influence the behavior of both libraries managing the click events. In our map view, we have to add the `data-tap-disabled` directive to disable click event management by Ionic and allow `angular-google-maps`, and thus Google Maps to do its own event management.

ui-gmap-google-map

Next up is the `ui-gmap-google-map` directive. This is the wrapping element that actually initiates Google Maps. For Trendicity, we have used three configuration attributes of this directive: control, center, and zoom.

```
// /www/templates/tap-map.html
<ui-gmap-google-map
  control="map.control"
  center="map.center"
  zoom="map.zoom">

  <!-- contents -->
</ui-gmap-google-map>
```

`control` is an empty object that will be extended with functionality by `angular-google-maps` once the map has been initialized. The two functions added are `getGMap()`, which returns the direct reference of the Google map instance being used by the directive, and `refresh(optionalCoords({latitude:, longitude})`, which refreshes the current map on its current coords if no coords are specified.

`center` is an object or array containing a latitude and longitude to center the map on. By default we will try to center the map on the user's current location using the `GeolocationService.getCurrentPosition()` method.

`zoom` is an expression to evaluate as the map's zoom level.

ui-gmap-markers

With the main `ui-gmap-google-map` directive properly configured, the next order of business is to add markers to the map. Thankfully, `angular-google-maps` contains another helpful directive that allows you to efficiently manage multiple map markers via AngularJS -`ui-gmap-markers`. This directive is not to be confused with the `ui-gmap-marker` directive (singular marker).

Since Trendicity's map view will be displaying several markers, using the plural `markers` directive is more efficient because it has been designed to overcome the high overhead of using `ng-repeat` with the singular `marker` directive. The four configuration options for this directive - models, coords, icon, and click - are shown below.

```
// /www/templates/tap-map.html
<ui-gmap-markers
    models="map.markers"
    coords="'coords'"
    icon="'icon'"
    click="'showPost'">
</ui-gmap-markers>
```

`models` is an array of objects defining each marker to add to the map. It is worth mentioning that each model object in the array must contain an identifier property, which will be seen when constructing the `map.markers` array in the map view Controller section below.

`coords` is the name (string) of the property of the model in the models array containing the marker coordinates, and must refer to an object containing `latitude` and `longitude` properties, or a **GeoJSON Point** object. The special value `'self'` can be used to tell the directive that the objects in the array directly contain the marker coordinate object values.

`icon` is the name (string) of the property of the model in the models array containing the URL to the icon image to use for each marker.

`click` can be a string or expression defining the event handler to be executed when clicking a marker. In this case, a string is used to define the name of the handler function on the marker model.

Overriding the Nav Bar

Before continuing onto the Map View Controller, it is worth mentioning that the map view's template file also contains an `ion-nav-bar` that overrides the one defined for all tabs inside the `www/templates/home.html` file. The reason for this is that allowing users to search for posts that are trending or from their personal feed doesn't make as much sense on the map view since discovery is directly tied to the location pin.

Instead, two new buttons are used on the right side of the nav bar - one for refreshing the view after the pin's location has changed and another for repositioning the pin on the user's current location. To accomplish this task, a new `ion-nav-bar` directive (shown below) is placed inside the `ion-view` and outside the `ion-content`.

```
// /www/templates/tap-map.html
<ion-nav-bar>
    <ion-nav-buttons side="left">
        <button menu-toggle="left" class="button button-icon
icon ion-navicon"></button>
    </ion-nav-buttons>
    <ion-nav-buttons side="right">
        <button class="button button-icon icon ion-refresh"
ng-click="refresh()"></button>
        <button class="button button-icon icon ion-pinpoint"
ng-click="locate()"></button>
    </ion-nav-buttons>
</ion-nav-bar>
```

Map View Controller

That wraps up the HTML for the map view inside of the map tab. We have seen how to force Ionic not to handle taps and clicks inside of our map by using the `data-tap-disabled` directive, covered the setup of the two directives provided by the `angular-google-maps` library, and discussed how to override the map view's default nav bar. In this section, we will explore the implementation of the `MapViewCtrl` and learn how easy it can be to manage Google Map components from AngularJS.

Initializing the Controller

When the `MapViewCtrl` first loads, it has to initialize the `$scope.map` object which contains the necessary information to configure the two 'angular-google-maps' directives discussed above. In addition, the `uiGmapGoogleMapApi` service, which returns a promise that is resolved with the current `google.maps` object when the SDK is ready, is used to ensure that the map has finished loading. It is also bound to the appropriate controls before triggering a call to `$scope.refresh()` or `$scope.locate()`. All this logic is wrapped inside the handler for the `$ionicView.enter` event so that the map can be updated with the most recent initial location each time the view comes into focus.

```
// /www/js/controllers/map.js
$scope.map = {
  zoom: 15,
  center: GeolocationService.getDefaultPosition(),
  control: {},
  markers: []
};

$scope.$on('$ionicView.enter', function() {
  $ionicHistory.clearHistory();
  $ionicSideMenuDelegate.canDragContent(false);

  uiGmapGoogleMapApi.then(function(maps) {
    if ($stateParams.latitude && $stateParams.longitude) {
      $scope.map.center = $stateParams;
      uiGmapGoogleMapApi.then(function(maps) {
        $scope.refresh($stateParams);
      });
    } else {
      $timeout(function(){
        var options = {
          timeout: 10000,
          maximumAge: 600000,
          enableHighAccuracy: false
        };
        $scope.locate(options);
      });
    }
  });
});
```

`$timeout` is used to delay execution until the end of the current `$digest` cycle.

Refreshing Posts

In order to allow users the ability to refresh the map view with new Instagram posts when the pin's location changes, the `$scope.refresh()` function, shown below, was created. At this point, the `$scope.map.control` object has been populated by the `angular-google-maps` library since it was passed as a configuration option of the `ui-gmap-google-map` directive, allowing the `getGMap()` function to be called to access the latitude and longitude of the map's center. This is used to create a position object that is passed to the `findNearby-`

Posts() function of the PostsService in order to retrieve a new set of Instagram posts centered on the location pin.

Once the posts are available, a new array of marker objects is created. Each individual marker object contains the coords, id, title, icon, and data properties, as well as a showPost() function. These object properties are required for the configuration of the ui-gmap-markers that was described above. Finally, the $scope.map.markers variable is updated with the new array of marker objects, so that the map view can be properly refreshed with nearby Instagram posts.

```
// /www/js/controllers/map.js
$scope.refresh = function(position) {
  var pinPos = position || {
    latitude: $scope.map.control.getGMap().getCenter().lat(),
    longitude: $scope.map.control.getGMap().getCenter().lng()
  };
  PostsService.findNearbyPosts(pinPos).then(function (posts)
{
    var markers = [];
    _.each(posts, function (post) {
      var image = {
        url: post.images.thumbnail.url,
        scaledSize: new google.maps.Size(20,20),
        origin: new google.maps.Point(0,0)
      };
      var marker = {
        coords: post.location,
        id: post.id,
        title: post.link,
        icon: image,
        data: post
      };
      marker.showPost = function() {
        $scope.showPost(post);
      };
      markers.push(marker);
    });
    $scope.map.markers = markers;
  });
};
```

Locating the User

With the refresh button in the nav bar linked to the $scope.refresh() function via an ng-click, the next order of business is to create the

`$scope.locate()` function so that users can reposition the pin on their current location. This function is very straightforward and simply involves using the `getCurrentPosition()` function of the `GeolocationService` before updating the `$scope.map.center` variable. Invoking the `$scope.refresh()` function with the user's current position object will take care of updating the map with nearby Instagram posts.

```
// /www/js/controllers/map.js
$scope.locate = function (options) {
  $ionicLoading.show();
  GeolocationService.getCurrentPosition(options).then(
    function (position) {
      $scope.map.center = position.coords;
      $scope.map.control.refresh(position.coords);
      $scope.refresh(position.coords);
      $ionicLoading.hide();
    },
    function() {
      $ionicLoading.hide();
    }
  );
};
```

Displaying Posts

Now that the user can refresh the map with new Instagram posts and reposition themselves back to their original location, all that is left is to give them the ability to view a larger version of the post when they click on a marker's image. This is accomplished by using the `$ionicPopup` service from within the `$scope.showPost()` function that is invoked when a marker is clicked.

The implementation is straightforward and begins by updating the `$scope.currentPost` variable with the `post` object that is passed into the function. A few configuration properties are set, and then an array of `buttons` is defined. The `PostsService.likePost()` function is used inside the `onTap` event handler for the Like button to allow users to like new posts directly from the map view. The full configuration of the `$ionicPopup` service is shown below.

```
// /www/js/controllers/map.js
$scope.showPost = function(post) {
  $scope.currentPost = post;
  var postPopup = $ionicPopup.show({
```

```
      templateUrl: 'templates/popups/post.html',
      scope: $scope,
      cssClass: 'popup-full',
      buttons: [{
        text: 'Like',
        type: 'button-light',
        onTap: function(e) {
          e.preventDefault();

          // Like this post
          if (!post.user_has_liked) {
            PostsService.likePost(post.id)
              .success(function () {
                console.log('you liked it!');
              });
          } else {
            console.log('you already liked it previously!');
          }
        }
      }, {
        text: 'Cancel',
        type: 'button-light',
        onTap: function(e) {
          $scope.currentPost = null;
          return true;
        }
      }]
    });
  };
```

Specifying the `templateUrl` and `cssClass` properties of the configuration object in the above call to `$ionicPopup.show()` allows you to override the default look and feel of the popup. Data from the `$scope.currentPost` object is used to create a simple view, but notice that no button markup was included in the template since buttons are handled entirely by the `$ionicPopup` service.

```
// /www/templates/popups/post.html
<div class="list">
  <div class="item item-avatar">
    <img ng-src="{{currentPost.user.profile_picture}}">
    <h2>{{currentPost.user.username}}</h2>
    <p>{{currentPost.caption.text}}</p>
  </div>

  <div class="item item-image">
    <img ng-
```

```
src="{{currentPost.images.standard_resolution.url}}">
  </div>
</div>
```

Loading a Favorite Location

You may have noticed that inside the `$ionicView.enter` event handler there was a check to see if `$stateParams.latitude` and `$stateParams.longitude` were defined. If they are present, the `MapViewCtrl` sets the map's center to those coordinates and invokes `$scope.refresh()` to load the Instagram posts near that location.

The reason these parameters are available via the `$stateParams` service is because the `/map` route, which was defined in the `www/js/app.js` file, had its `url` property set to `'/map/?latitude&longitude'`. This is the proper syntax for defining query parameters that will be parsed and made available by the `$stateParams` service.

Summary

In this chapter you have seen how to leverage the `angular-google-maps` library and ngCordova's `$cordovaGeolocation` service to create a fully functional map view that displays Instagram posts near a desired location. Along the way, you made updates to the `GeolocationService`, learned how to disable Ionic click event management, configured various `angular-google-maps` directives, and implemented the `MapViewCtrl`. This chapter has provided you with the necessary tools and examples to facilitate the integration of an interactive map in your future Ionic projects.

Authentication 7

Authentication is a common problem that just about every developer faces at some point in their career. Since security is such a major concern these days, it is often solved early on in the project. Using third-party libraries can often help solve this problem. In some cases, an OAuth-based approach can be used. In other cases, this may not be an option depending upon how much control the developer has over the backend.

We would like to make authentication as seamless as possible for Trendicity. We don't want the user to perform an action, get prompted to login, enter their credentials, be taken to a home page, and then perform the same set of steps again. Then it could be possible that their request is rejected due to authentication. We can do better than that.

Since *Ionic* uses AngularJS, we can incorporate the **angular-http-auth** library (created by Witold Szczerba) to help us solve this problem. We can use this library when using an OAuth based approach, or when using a traditional token-based authentication scheme.

Desired user experience

We would like to have a more transparent authentication solution where the user can be taken to a login page whenever an HTTP request fails due to not being authenticated. Then after the user logs in, we want to proceed as if the user had been logged in the whole time. This can be useful, especially when the backend service expires a token after a certain amount of time.

You can see this feature first hand in the **Trendicity** application by selecting the *Search* icon at the top-right portion of the application. Just make sure you are not already logged in. You can logout by selecting the side menu *Logout* option.

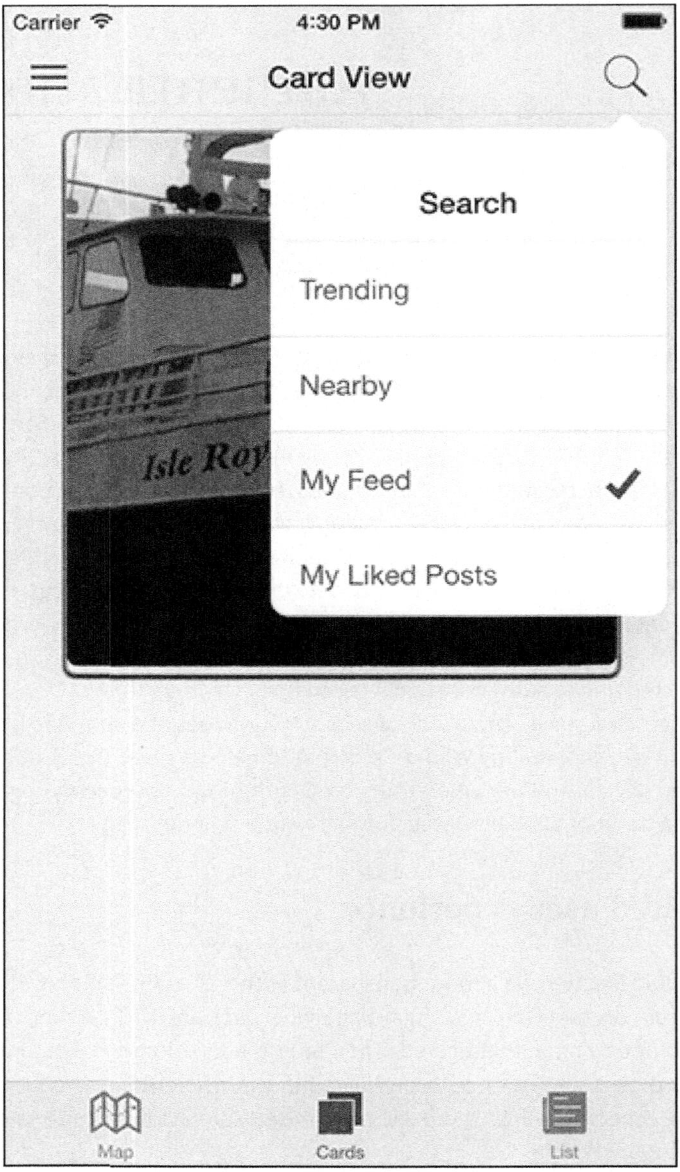

Upon selecting the *My Feed* option in the `$ionicPopover`, you will be prompted to login.

Upon selecting *Login to Instagram*, you will be presented with an Instagram login window.

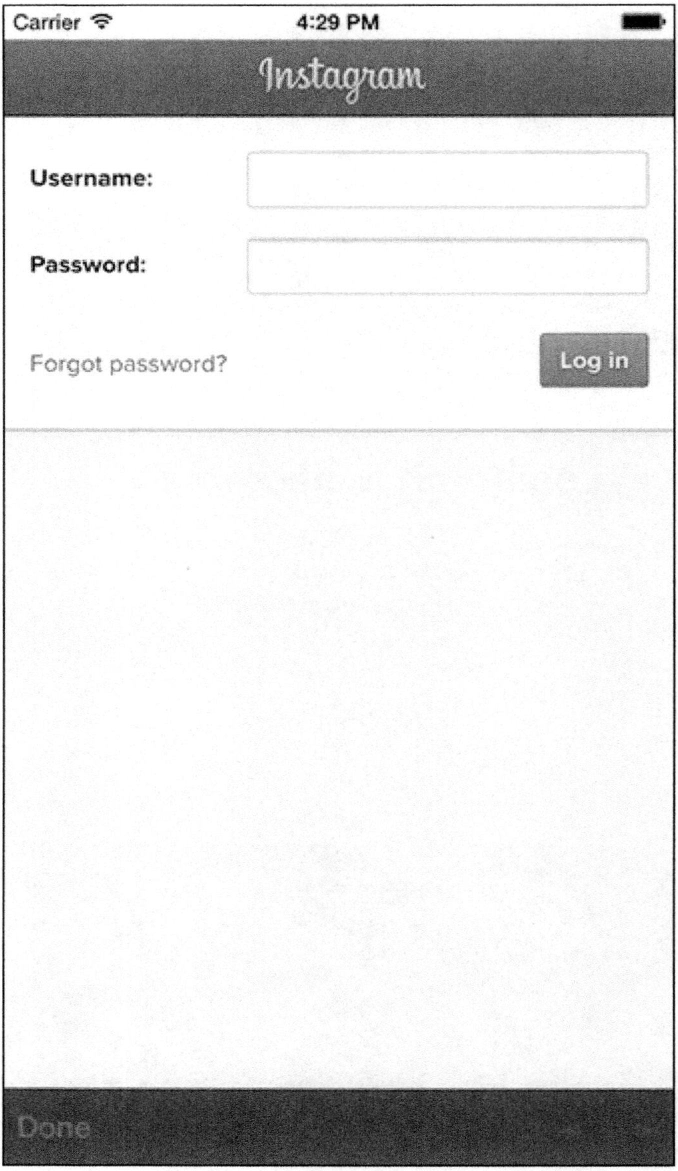

Once you successfully login, the HTTP request to retrieve the *My Feed* posts will be present. Only, this time it will have the `access_token` appended to the URL parameters. You should now see the photos for your user feed.

Incorporating angular-http-auth

A common practice for backend services is to issue an HTTP status code of 401 when a request needs to be authenticated. The `angular-http-auth` library implements an angular service called `authService` using an `HttpInterceptor`. This service will intercept HTTP requests and detect an HTTP status code of 401. The `authService` will then broadcast the event `event:auth-loginRequired`. We can then listen for this event and prompt the user to login.

OAuth2 based approach

In the case of Instagram, it doesn't return an HTTP status code of 401 when a request fails due to authentication. Instead, it returns an HTTP status of 400, which is a generic error code indicating a "Bad Request." In addition to that, it returns an error type. In the **Trendicity** application, we are going to have the `TrendicityInterceptor` in `www/js/services/interceptors.js` look for this condition.

```
responseError: function(rejection) {
  if (rejection.status == 400  &&
      rejection.data.meta.error_type ==
        'OAuthParameterException') {
    console.log("detected an Instagram auth error...");
    // Set status to 401 and let the authService handle it
    rejection.status = 401;
  }
  return $q.reject(rejection);
}
```

If we find this condition, we are going to set the HTTP status code to 401 and let the *angular-http-auth* `authService` handle this. Since that service will raise the event `event:auth-loginRequired` we can listen for this event in `www/js/controllers/app.js`.

```
// Handle the login required event raised by the authService
$scope.$on('event:auth-loginRequired', function() {
  console.log('handling event:auth-loginRequired...');
  $scope.loginModal.show();
});
```

When the event `event:auth-loginRequired` is triggered, we show an `ionicModal` to prompt the user to *Login with Instagram*. If the user chooses to *Login with Instagram*, we will display a window with the external Instagram login URL. The Trendicity application does not process the username and password directly.

Below are some code snippets from the `www/js/services/instagram.js` `login()` function. Once the user logs into Instagram, we inform the *angular-http-auth* `authService` that the user has in fact logged in successfully. The `authService` will then apply the `configUpdater` function on any pending HTTP requests. In this case, it will resend the previous unauthorized requests with our `access_token` added as a parameter. The success/error/finally blocks for those original HTTP requests will then be executed appropriately as if the user was already authenticated.

```
this.login = function() {
  var configUpdater = function(config) {
    config.params = config.params || {};
    config.params.access_token = self.getAccessToken();
    return config;
  }

  if (self.isLoggedIn()) {
    authService.loginConfirmed(null, configUpdater);
  }
}
```

Token-based approach

Token-based authentication (non-OAuth) is a common way of authenticating directly between a trusted client and server. In this case, you would display a traditional login page where the user is prompted for their username and password. The main difference here is that your application is collecting the username and password directly. Whereas with OAuth, you are redirecting to a URL that you do not own.

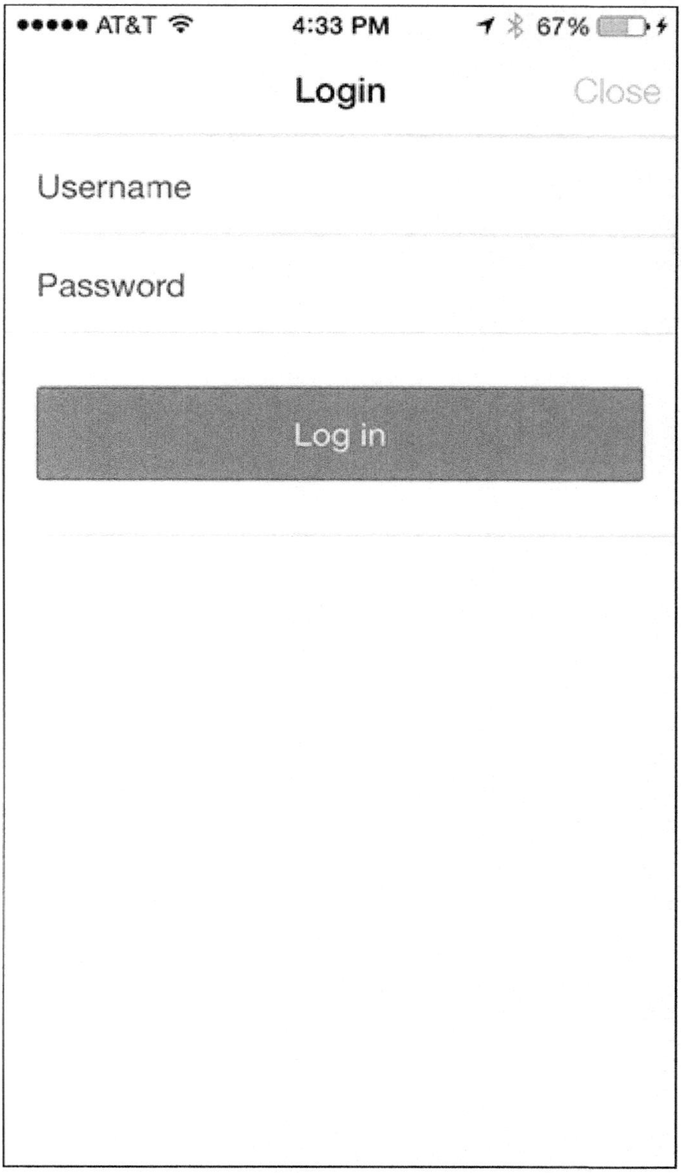

In this scenario, the user enters their username and password and submits the form. Below is the HTML needed to create the login modal.

```
<div class="modal">
  <ion-header-bar>
    <h1 class="title">Login</h1>
    <div class="buttons">
      <button class="button button-clear"
              ng-click="closeLogin()">Close</button>
    </div>
  </ion-header-bar>
  <ion-content>
    <div style="color:red">${{message}}</div>
    <form ng-submit="doLogin()">
      <div class="list">
        <label class="item item-input">
          <span class="input-label">Username</span>
          <input type="text" ng-model="loginData.username">
        </label>
        <label class="item item-input">
          <span class="input-label">Password</span>
          <input type="password" ng-
model="loginData.password">
        </label>
        <label class="item">
          <button class="button button-block button-positive"
                  type="submit">Log in</button>
        </label>
      </div>
    </form>
  </ion-content>
</div>
```

You can now load the HTML for the modal in a controller using the code below.

```
$ionicModal.fromTemplateUrl('templates/login.html', {
  scope: $scope,
  animation: 'slide-in-up'
}).then(function(modal) {
  $scope.loginModal = modal;
});
```

When the form is submitted, the `doLogin` function will be called. In this scenario, we would issue a post request to a backend server with the username and password entered by the user. Because this is a login request, we set the header attribute `ignoreAuthModule` to true. This attribute will tell the *angular-http-auth* `authService` to bypass the normal intercepting of HTTP status codes. If the login request fails, we don't want to misinterpret that as a normal request that needs to be authenticated. Basically, this is a non-authenticated request.

```
this.doLogin = function(username, password) {
  $http.post('https://hostname/login',
    { username: username, password: password },
    { ignoreAuthModule: true })
  .success(function (data, status, headers, config) {

    $http.defaults.headers.common.Authorization =
                              data.authorizationToken;

    var configUpdater = function(config) {
      config.headers.Authorization = data.authorizationToken;
      return config;
    }

    authService.loginConfirmed(data, configUpdater);
  })
  .error(function (data, status, headers, config) {
    $rootScope.$broadcast('event:auth-login-failed', status);
  });
}
```

If the login request is successful, we add the `authorizationToken` to the default set of headers. This is done so that future requests will be authenticated. Then we inform the `authService` that login has been confirmed. We pass in a function that will be responsible for adding the `authorizationToken` to the headers of any previously pending HTTP requests.

If the login request receives an error, we broadcast the event `event:auth-login-failed` on the `$rootScope`. We can then listen for this event and use it to display an error message on the `ionicModal` used to login.

```
$scope.$on('event:auth-login-failed', function(e, status) {
  var error = "Login failed.";
  if (status == 401) {
    error = 'Invalid Username or Password.";
  }
  $scope.message = error;
});
```

Also, since the *angular-http-auth* `authService` will raise the event `event:auth-loginConfirmed`, you can do something when that event occurs, if necessary. For instance, you can hide the `ionicModal`. In the case of Trendicity, we don't need to do anything, since we are using OAuth 2.0 to authenticate with Instagram.

```
// Handle the login confirmed event raised by the authService
$scope.$on('event:auth-loginConfirmed', function() {
  console.log('handling event:auth-loginConfirmed...');
  $scope.loginModal.hide();
});
```

Cancel login

If the user decides not to login when prompted to, and decides to close the login modal, you need to inform the *angular-http-auth* `authService` of this. That way, any pending HTTP requests can be cancelled. For example, in `www/js/controllers/app.js`, you have the `closeLogin` function.

```
// Triggered in the login modal to close it
$scope.closeLogin = function() {
  InstagramService.loginCancelled();
  $scope.loginModal.hide();
};
```

The `authService` will also raise the event `event:auth-loginCancelled`. You can then setup a watch on the event in case you want to do something when that occurs. In the case of the Trendicity application, we don't need to do anything extra.

Summary

In this chapter you learned how to make use of the third-party `angular-http-auth` library to help streamline the login process in an Ionic application. You learned how this library can be used with both an OAuth2 approach, as well as with a traditional token-based approach. In the next chapter, you will learn how to design an application and take advantage of some built-in Ionic styles and components that will make your application more appealing to the end user.

Instagram Service 8

To do just about anything of interest in a mobile web application, you have to integrate with a backend service. The **Trendicity** application is no different. We need to be able to retrieve photos (aka posts) from Instagram and provide them to the application. Trendicity integrates with Instagram through the **Instagram API**. Since a layered application is desireable, the interactions with Instagram are placed inside an angular `Service`. You can find the Trendicity `InstagramService` in the `www/js/services/instagram.js` file.

To retrieve information from the Instagram API, you must first obtain a `client_id` by setting up an Instagram client using **Instagram Manage Clients**. In order for the application to make Instagram API requests when running in a desktop browser, we will need to find a solution to a **CORS** issue. We don't want to have to deploy the app to a device/simulator every time we want to test something.

The Instagram API allows for two different types of requests: non-authenticated and authenticated. Once you have a `client_id`, you can make non-authenticated requests like `Popular Posts` and `Nearby Posts`. To make authenticated requests, you must authenticate the user using the OAuth 2.0 protocol.

For retrieving popular posts or nearby posts, a non-authenticated request can be made by just using the `client_id`. For retrieving a user's feed, a user's liked posts, or for liking/disliking a post, an authenticated request must be made. Also, note there are different **Limits** placed on non-authenticated versus authenticated requests.

Authentication

The Instagram API provides two types of OAuth 2.0 authentication: Server Side authentication and Client Side authentication. We will be using the Client Side authentication approach in our mobile application. We will need to open a window with the Instagram login URL. The user will provide Instagram with their username and password, then submit the form. Instagram will redirect to a URL that we provide. This URL will contain an `access_token`. We can then use this `access_token` to make authenticated requests.

Login

The Trendicity application never sees the user's actual credentials (username and password) because the application just opens a window with the Instagram login URL. But to do that, we need to provide some parameters.

- client_id - this is the client id that is setup using **Instagram Manage Clients**
- redirect_uri - this is the redirect url that was setup using **Instagram Manage Clients**
- scope - the user permissions being requested
- response_type - this will be set to "token" for client side authentication

Below is a slightly modified code snippet from the `InstagramService login()` function. Although a `client_id` has been provided, you are encouraged to setup your own.

```
var CLIENT_ID = '75d27c9457cd4d1abbacf80a228f4a10';
var AUTH_URL = 'https://instagram.com/oauth/authorize';
var AUTH_REDIRECT_URL = 'http://localhost:8100/
instagram.html';

var loginWindow = window.open(AUTH_URL
  + '?client_id=' + CLIENT_ID
  + '&scope=likes+comments&response_type=token&redirect_uri='
  + AUTH_REDIRECT_URL, '_blank',

'width=400,height=250,location=no,clearsessioncache=yes,clearcache=yes
);
```

We will need to take a slightly different approach depending on whether the application is running on a device/simulator or on a desktop browser. To help us detect this, we can use the `ionic.Platform.isWebView()` function.

DEVICE/SIMULATOR

To open a window in a Cordova-based application, we need to use the `InAppBrowser` Cordova plugin to open a new window with the Instagram login URL. This allows us to use the standard `window.open()` function.

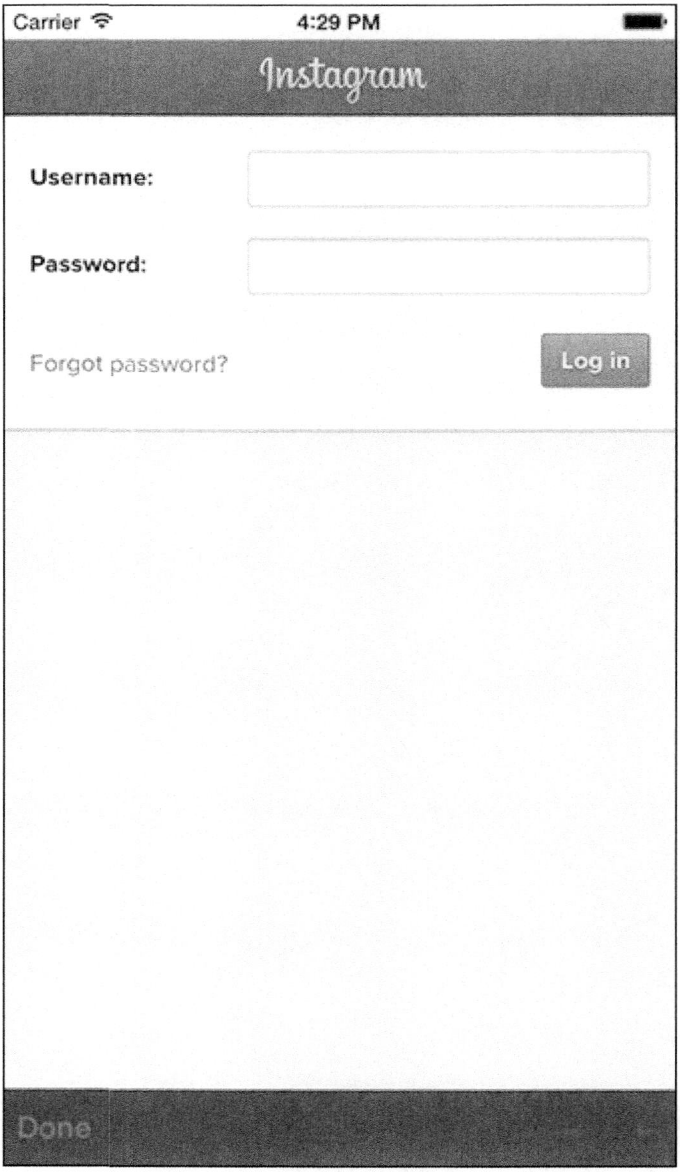

After the window has been opened, we check to see if we are running in a *WebView* (i.e. device/simulator). If we are, then we add an `InAppBrowswer` specific `loadstart` event listener to the window. When the user logs in, the URL will change to the redirect URL (due to the Instagram redirect) that we provided, and we can parse the URL for the access_token. Once we have the access_token, we persist it using the localStorageService and then we close the window.

```
if (ionic.Platform.isWebView()) {
  loginWindow.addEventListener('loadstart', function (event)
{
    if ((event.url).indexOf(AUTH_REDIRECT_URL) === 0) {
      var accessToken = (event.url).split('access_token=')
[1];
      localStorageService.set('accessToken', accessToken);
      loginWindow.close();
    }
  });
}
```

You may have noticed that the AUTH_REDIRECT_URL was defined as http://localhost:8100/instagram.html. You might be wondering how this URL would be accessed from the mobile application. On a device/simulator, this page will not be found. Had we not closed the window, we would have gotten a 404 page not found error. However, we don't really care. We just want to get the access_token from the URL itself. Actually, we could have made the AUTH_REDIRECT_URL whatever we wanted to as long as it matches the redirect URL that was defined in the Instagram Manage Clients setup site. We just defined it using localhost so that we can take advantage of that when running the application in a desktop browser.

DESKTOP BROWSER

Since we can't use a Cordova plugin on the browser, we are going to have to take a slightly different approach. The window.open() function will just open a new browser window as you would expect.

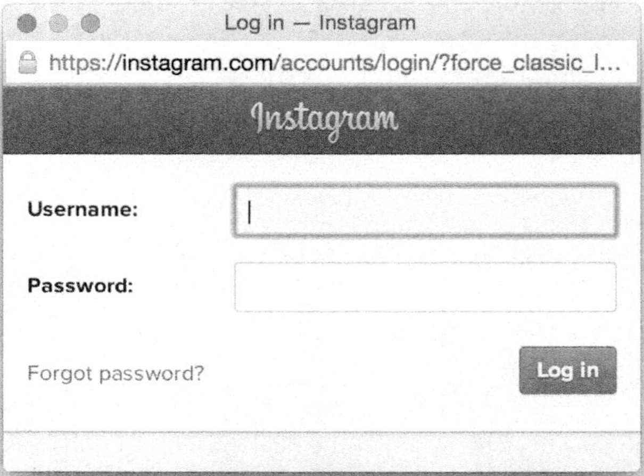

Here we could try to add a `beforeunload` or `unload` event listener on the window to try to achieve the same behavior as we did with the `WebView` scenario. However, those approaches are very problematic and lead to several issues. They don't work consistently across browers. Also, there are problems when the user enters the wrong username or password. Since this is not going to be executed in our production environment, we aren't overly concerned about this code. We just want to be able to login when running on the desktop browser. In other words, we are going to create a "hack," strictly for development purposes.

```
if (ionic.Platform.isWebView()) {
  // omitted for brevity
} else { // running on a desktop browser
  var intervalCount = 0;
  var timesToRepeat = 100;
  var intervalDelay = 3000; // in ms

  var loginPoller = function(event) {
    intervalCount++;
    if (self.isLoggedIn()) {
      console.log('user is logged in now');
      $interval.cancel(promise);
```

```
      } else {
        if (intervalCount >= timesToRepeat) {
          $interval.cancel(promise);
          loginWindow.close();
        }
      }
    };
    var promise =
      $interval(loginPoller, intervalDelay, timesToRepeat,
  false);
    }
  };
```

The approach makes use of an `$interval`, which is similar to using `setInterval` in JavaScript. Instead of returning an interval id, `$interval` returns a promise. After the login window is opened, we are going to keep calling the `loginListener()` function every 3 seconds, until either the user is logged in or we have exhausted the maximum number of times to repeat. If the user logs in, we just cancel the interval. If we reach the maximum number of times to repeat, in addition to cancelling the interval, we close the window.

If the user logs in, the browser will be redirected to the `AUTH_REDIRECT_URL`, which was defined as `http://localhost:8100/instagram.html` as depicted below.

```
<!DOCTYPE html>
<html>
<head></head>
<script>
  function obtainAccessToken() {
    var accessToken = location.href.split('access_token=')
[1];
    localStorage.setItem('ls.accessToken', accessToken);
    window.close();
  }
</script>
<body onload="obtainAccessToken()">
  This is just a hack for getting the access token when
using a desktop browser.
</body>
</html>
```

This `instagram.html` page will allow us to obtain the `access_token` from the redirect URL. Similar to what we did in the previous section, we persist the token to `localStorage`. Only this time, we need to prefix the accessToken with 'ls' since that is what the angularLocalStorage uses as a default prefix. Once we process the access_token we can close the window.

Logout

When the user requests to logout, we are going to attempt to log the user out of Instagram. Since the Instagram API doesn't provide a mechanism for this, we are going to attempt to mimic the logout request on their website.

```
this.logout = function() {
  var promise = ionic.Platform.isWebView() ?
$http.post(LOGOUT_URL) : $http.jsonp(LOGOUT_URL);
  promise.error(function (data, status) {
    console.log('logout returned status:' + status);
  })
  .finally(function() {
    localStorageService.remove('accessToken');
  });
  return promise;
};
```

You may be wondering why the access_token is not being passed here. When the user logs into Instagram, a cookie is stored in the browser by Instagram. By making this logout request, Instagram will remove the cookie that was stored in the browser. We could just remove the access_token instead of making the logout request. However, this errors on the side of caution since security is a very touchy area these days. If a user requests to logout, then we really want to log them out. If we didn't make the logout request, and the user tried to login again, the cookie would be used and the the user would not have to provide any credentials direcly.

To avoid a **CORS** issue when running on a desktop browser, we are going to use a JSONP request. We won't have a CORS issue when running on a device/simulator. Due to the nature of the response from Instagram, we expect to get a 404 when running on a desktop browser. Regardless, if the request is successful or not, we still remove the accessToken from localStorage.

CORS

Several people in the *Ionic* community have struggled in the past with **CORS** issues when using a desktop browser to develop/test with. On the device/simulator, CORS is not an issue since you can whitelist origins in the Cordova provided config.xml. You can use an asterisk to leave it wide open. Or for tighter security, you can specify the origins that are allowed to be accessed.

```
<access origin="*" />
```

In some cases, you may have control over your backend and can **enable CORS**. However, in other cases, you may not have control over the backend. In our case, we are working on an Instagram mashup and have no control over the backend. The most recommended solution for this is to use Chrome and disable web security. This is very limiting. What if a developer wants to use Firefox or some other browser for that matter? Also, what if the user really doesn't want to hijack their browser and compromise security? Another soluton is use JSONP, which Instagram supports. The problem with that is it is limited to GET requests, and the error handling is quirky since you always get back an HTTP status of 200 when an actual error occurs. We need to issue POST and DELETE requests so JSONP won't work for us either. Fortunately, the Ionic CLI has a feature that we can leverage to solve this problem in a very elegant way.

When developing/testing using a desktop browser, you should be using the `ionic serve` command which is part of the `ionic-cli` (see Chapter 3: Development environment, tooling and workflow for more details). When the `ionic-serve` command is executed, it will launch an HTTP server. We can take advantage of an `ionic serve` feature that allows for a proxy server to be configured. So requests for a particular URL path can we be treated as if they were in the same domain. To do this, we define the proxy in the `ionic.project` file in the root directory of the Trendicity application.

```
{
  "name": "trendicity",
  "app_id": "",
  "proxies": [
  {
    "path": "/instagram/api",
    "proxyUrl": "https://api.instagram.com/v1"
```

```
    }
    ]
  }
```

So anytime our application makes an HTTP request to "/instagram/api", the proxy server will use the "proxyUrl" instead. In this case, it will use "**https://api.instagram.com/v1**". Any parameters that are passed to "/instagram/api" will be passed to the "proxyUrl". As far as the browser is concerned, the request is not considered to be a cross-domain request.

So in the `InstagramService`, we define our `API_ENDPOINT` based on whether the application is running in a `WebView` or in a desktop browser. If running in a desktop browser, we take advantage of our proxy server and let `ionic serve` do its magic. If the app is running in the *WebView* (aka Cordova), we just use the actual Instagram url since Cordova does not enforce the CORS restriction.

```
var API_ENDPOINT = ionic.Platform.isWebView()
  ? 'https://api.instagram.com/v1' : '/instagram/api';
```

Non-Authenticated Requests

For non-authenticated requests, like `Popular Posts` and `Nearby Posts` we must pass a `client_id`. A `client_id` can obtained by setting up an Instagram client using **Instagram Manage Clients**.

Below is an example of the `Popular Posts` request. The `Nearby Posts` is very similar.

```
var API_ENDPOINT = ionic.Platform.isWebView()
  ? 'https://api.instagram.com/v1' : '/instagram/api';

// Code omitted for brevity

this.findPopularPosts = function(options) {
  options = options || {};
  options.client_id = CLIENT_ID;

  var promise =
    $http.get(API_ENDPOINT + '/media/popular', {
      params: options
    })
    .error(function(data, status) {
      console.log('findPopularPosts returned status:' +
status);
```

```
    });
    return promise;
  };
```

In addition to adding the `client_id` as an parameter, we allow for an `options` object to be passed in. We do this to be consistent with some of the other functions in the service where additional parameters can be passed. In the future, Instagram may add additional parameters to this endpoint. If so, we don't need to change this function since it already allows additional parameters to be passed using the `options` object.

If the user has been authenticated, we should still pass the `access_token` as well. The reason being that non-authenticated requests have much stricter **access limits** on them.

Authenticated Requests

For authenticated requests, like `User Feed`, `Liked Posts`, `Like Post` and `Dislike Post`, we need to pass an `access_token`. Since we want to pass the `access_token` on both non-authenticated and authenticated requests, we can do that in an angular `HttpInterceptor`. Below is a simplified code snippet from the `TrendicityInterceptor` in the `www/js/services/interceptors.js` file.

```
  request: function(config) {
    // Handle adding the access_token for instagram api
  requests
    var InstagramService = $injector.get('InstagramService');
    if (InstagramService.isLoggedIn() &&
        config.url.indexOf(InstagramService.getEndpoint()) ===
  0) {
      config.params = config.params || {};
      config.params.access_token =
  InstagramService.getAccessToken();
    }
    return config;
  },
```

Here we inject the `InstagramService` as to avoid a circular dependency. Once we have that, we check to see if the user is logged in and the HTTP request is for the Instagram `API_ENDPOINT`. If so, we add the `access_token` to the config.params.

Notice, for example, in the `likePost()` function we don't have pass the `access_token`. All we need to do here is pass in the `mediaId` as part of the endpoint url.

```
this.likePost = function(mediaId) {
  var promise =
    $http.post(API_ENDPOINT + '/media/' + mediaId + '/likes')
    .error(function (data, status) {
      console.log('likePost returned status:' + status);
  });
  return promise;
};
```

Summary

So now you should be more familiar with how the Instagram API works and how the Trendicity `InstagramService` interacts with it. You were introduced to an `ionic serve` feature to get around CORS issues when making cross-origin HTTP requests from a desktop browser. You learned a useful "hack" to allow you to login to Instagram from a desktop browser. You have learned that in order for an application to talk to Instagram, you must first setup an Instagram client so that you can obtain a `client_id`. This `client_id` is then used to make non-authenticated requests. You know how to automatically add the `access_token` parameter to all Instagram related HTTP requests using an Angular `HttpInterceptor`.

If you haven't noticed by now, *Ionic* is more than just a framework, it is really more of a hybrid mobile application development ecosystem. In the next chapter, you will learn what's coming next.

What's next? 9

Many developers appreciated Ionic when it launched because it offered a reasonable alternative to native development. As Ionic evolved, it has become a complete SDK for the creation of great hybrid mobile experiences on iOS and Android. The Ionic team consistently adds helpful tools and services to the SDK, such as updated libraries, platform-specific iconsets and new components. Ionic continues to expand its capability as a self-sustaining platform for hybrid mobile applications.

In this chapter, we will explore the present and near-future of what Ionic has in stock for the broader developer community.

Promoting your Ionic application

Getting the word out is a crucial step after having created an awesome application. To facilitate the marketability of developers' applications, Ionic has dedicated a section of its website to a showcase of applications built with the SDK.

Noteworthy Ionic applications to mention are *Songhop*, which lets you explore new music and is integrated with Spotify. Another example is *Sworkit*, an application designed for the fitness-conscious. You will also find *ChefSteps*, which enhances your ability to cook your own restaurant-worthy meals. Moreover, these applications have all been featured on Apple's App Store!

Clearly, hybrid mobile applications have come a long way since the introduction of smartphones, greatly propelled by Ionic's efforts, such that they have become on a par with their native counterparts.

Prototyping with Ionic Creator

Ionic has recently released the Ionic Creator, an online tool designed to let developers bootstrap their own applications more efficiently with an intuitive drag-and-drop interface. Once you're done, Creator lets you export your work as a fully functional, packaged Ionic application that you can build to run on mobile devices.

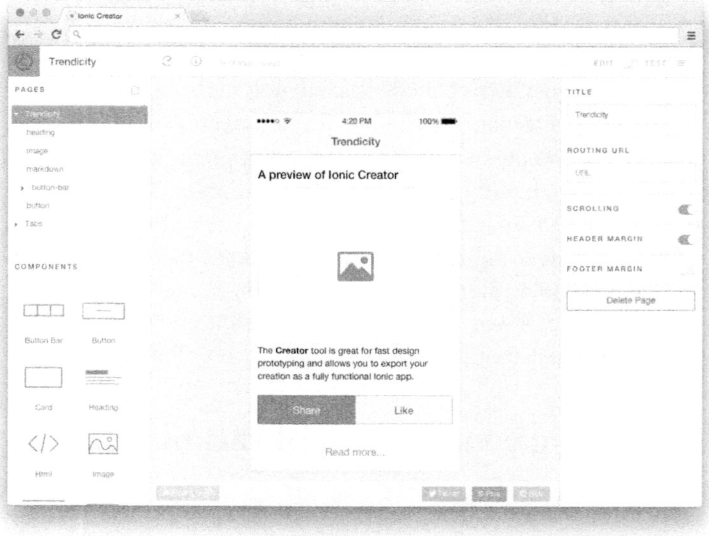

It's a great tool to quickly prototype interface designs before getting into the nitty-gritty of coding and styling your appliation. In fact, this tool is capable of rivaling other popular wireframing services the likes of Moqups, Invision and Mockup.io.

The advantage of designing with Creator is its inherent and seamless integration with the Ionic platform and its ability to create a fully functional application that is ready to be installed on your devices.

Ionic's evolution

With the introduction of new components such as action sheets, popovers, and slide box, we are witnessing an evolutionary progression in Ionic's featureset. Enhanced functionality in the form of performance-oriented components such as `collection-repeat`, scalable building blocks like `ion`-prefixed AngularJS directives, and its own iconset bearing the Ionicons name demonstrate that Ionic has evolved to become a complete SDK for hybrid mobile application development.

The platform boasts a robust collection of tools meant to facilitate the development of hybrid mobile applications.

Ionic CLI

The Ionic CLI has been getting a lot of attention lately. For instance, Ionic CLI can generate Android applications using Crosswalk, which takes advantage of bundling a Chrome webview resulting in significant performance improvements. This is particularly important as it opens the door for millions of Android users still running on versions 4.0 and up to have access to the latest performance improvements of the Chrome in-app browser.

Ionic View

Sharing your creations using the platform has been simplified with the introduction of Ionic View. The View app supports both iOS and Android platforms and allows you to run your apps on your devices without having to use TestFlight or Google Play beta testing services. Sharing your Ionic apps can be achieved by using the following CLI command: `$ ionic share [EMAIL]`, replacing `[EMAIL]` with the email of the beta tester you would like to invite. The Ionic View app is an example of how the team is expanding the variety of services that are wrapped around the platform itself.

AngularJS 2.0 Support

With the recent announcement of AngularJS 2.0, Ionic has confirmed its pledge to fully supporting the new version of the framework. In fact, Ionic 2.0 is expected to integrate the new Angular in its second iteration of the platform. The inclusion of AngularJS 2.0 will bring with it major performance improvements, a new component model making extending Ionic easier and allowing comprehensive interactions with your app's data.

ngCordova

In addition, interacting with popular Cordova plugins has been optimized to work with AngularJS with the help of the `ngCordova` module, which happens to be created by the team behind Ionic. This extension allows you to interact with many of Cordova's plugins, letting you access the device's camera, photos and geolocation, creating native push notifications and much more.

Ions

Extending the core Ionic SDK has been facilitated by the inclusion of `ions`. As described on the platform's website, `ions` are "a curated collection of useful addons, components, and UX interactions for extending Ionic." Integrating these extensions is handled by the Ionic CLI through the `add` command. For instance, to get the "Tinder" cards that we used in Trendicity, you could execute the following command in your terminal: `$ ionic add ionic-ion-tinder-cards`.

Other Tidbits

An area of interest that has been developing lately is the use of native scrolling, instead of the current JavaScript-based implementation. The addition of such a mechanism will greatly impact the smoothness when interacting with long lists of items.

Platform continuity is another aspect of Ionic apps that has been emphasized recently. In essence, the Ionic platform allows you to use common building blocks that are adapted aesthetically to follow guidelines of different mobile platforms. For instance, as we saw in the `Designing the application` chapter, Ionic's action sheets are styled differently on iOS compared to Android.

With the growing popularity of Ionic, the developer community has been hard at work building creative extensions that serve as enhancements to the framework's core. For instance, the Collide library serves as a native JavaScript animation engine for both mobile applications and the web. Similar to Facebook's Pop engine for iOS, Collide promises to greatly improve the state of animations in hybrid mobile applications.

Google's Material Design has also made waves in the mobile design world, leading to the creation of Angular Material. This library ports Material's web components to the AngularJS world. Since Ionic is built on top of AngularJS, this means that your applications can tap into the new design paradigms of Material.

Ionic as a platform

Given the numerous facets of the platform, Ionic's creators have decided to expand on its initial implementation by offering new sets of services specific for the hybrid mobile app community. Similar to other mobile platforms, Ionic will now be considered a platform in itself. The mission now is to match what native SDKs offer, ranging from analytics to push notifications. The platform will integrate A/B testing, cross-platform push notifications, and pushing of new application releases automatically, bypassing the wait times of Apple's App Store and Google's Play Store.

A feature that has already been implemented is the aforementioned Ionic Creator. This tool is an indication of what we can expect in the near-future.

Moreover, "The Ionic Show," a monthly show dedicated to all things Ionic, is hosted by Drifty founders Max Lynch and Ben Sperry on YouTube. The hosts discuss updates to the Ionic SDK, showcase the latest and greatest Ionic-built applications, and taste new craft brews.

Following its first year of existence, Ionic has boasted over 400,000 applications created using the platform. Moreover, the platform is consistenly ranked in the top 50 most popular open source projects in the world, with over 15,000 stars on GitHub. A growing number of meetups have been organized in cities and countries around the world, bringing together Ionic developers and embracing the values of community openness. In order to further propel this trend, Ionic has published a keynote presentation perfect for presenting the platform to new developer communities. The team behind Ionic is also giving away free merchandise in the form of stickers and t-shirts for organizers of these local events.

Summary

In conclusion, Ionic began as a modest take on hybrid mobile applications, improving the way applications are created through the use of a framework. It has since flourished to become a complete software development platform with its own developer community, dedicated team and plethora of tools meant to facilitate newcomers and existing members with their application development.